CISTERCIAN FATHERS SERIES: NUMBER THIRTY-ONE

BERNARD OF CLAIRVAUX

ON THE
SONG OF SONGS III

CISTERCIAN FATHERS SERIES: NUMBER THIRTY-ONE

Bernard of Clairvaux
ON THE SONG OF SONGS III

translated by
KILIAN WALSH ocso
&
IRENE M. EDMONDS

Introduction by
EMERO STIEGMAN

Cistercian Publications
Kalamazoo, Michigan 49008
1979

The translation here presented is based on the critical Latin edition prepared by Jean Leclercq, H. M. Rochais, and C. H. Talbot under the sponsorship of the S. Order of Cistercians and published by Editiones Cistercienses, Piazza Tempio di Diana 14, I-00143 Rome.

© Cistercian Publications, 1979

First published 1979
by
Cistercian Publications, Inc.
Kalamazoo, Michigan 49008

Library of Congress Cataloging in Publication Data (Revised)

Bernard de Clairvaux, Saint, 1091?-1153.
   On the Song of Songs.

   (The Works of Bernard of Clairvaux, v. 2, 3)
(Cistercian Fathers series, no. 4, 7, 31)
   Vols. (2-) have imprint: Kalamazoo, Mich.,
Cistercian Publications.
   1. Bible. O.T. Song of Solomon—Sermons.
2. Sermons, Latin—Translations into English.
3. Sermons, English—Translations from Latin. I. Title.
II. Series: Bernard de Clairvaux, Saint, 1091?-1153.
Works. English. 1970. v. 2 [etc.]
BX890.B5 1970, vol.2, etc. [BS1485]   230'.2s
ISBN 0-87907-104-4   [223'.9'07]   73-168262

Book design by Gale Akins. Typeset at Humble Hills Graphics, Kalamazoo
Printed in the United States of America

CONTENTS

Cistercian Publications expresses its gratitude to the late Kilian Walsh, monk of Mount Melleray Abbey, for his unstinting generosity in translating the sermons of Saint Bernard on the Song of Songs, and to Irene M. Edmonds, who took up the task at Sermon Sixty-Three when Father Kilian's failing health forced him to give it up and who painstakingly matched her translation to his style.

ACTION AND CONTEMPLATION IN
SAINT BERNARD'S SERMONS
ON THE SONG OF SONGS

S AINT BERNARD thought of the Song of Songs as a 'contemplative discourse' (*theoricus sermo*), and in commenting upon it in his book of eighty-six sermons he described the ways of the contemplative.[1] It would not be difficult to draw from the literature of discussion on the action-contemplation issue a large body of opinion claiming the *Sermones super Cantica Canticorum* as a book for those who live the contemplative life, with the implication that those who live the active life would, of course, find such material too rich for their blood. Bernard himself did much to cast suspicion upon so awkward a division of christian experience into two lives. Had his masterpiece been surrendered to 'professionals', christian tradition would have been impoverished. To the contrary, no other spiritual work of the era has claimed as much attention for the influence it exercised upon the general piety of succeeding generations.

Today Bernard's text makes a claim beyond its sheer excellence and its historical position. In response to a broadening of the layperson's sense of christian responsibility, a new spirituality is under cultivation. Some of its proponents make striking assertions about its difference from classical schemes. It corrects, we are told, the unbiblical angelic anthropology of the medieval spiritual writers.[2] Even when the older spirituality is not so gravely misrepresented it may be slighted, the better to establish the appropriateness of the new.[3] It is as if, while arguing for *commitment* to the oppressed and *openness* to the vital moment, we were embarassed by the age-old ascetical-mystical categories. But, is it wise to relax in such small effort at understanding earlier generations of the Church? We may fear that crucial evidence of the Spirit's continuous presence will be obscured. A knowledge of St Bernard's *Super Cantica* is insurance against this hazard.

Let us admit immediately that the orientation of modern lay spirituality to an affirmation of the world, as we say, or to a building of human society will receive little encouragement from the Abbot of Clairvaux. His monastic vocation and monastic milieu gave him a different point of view on human experience. In the first of the sermons the author of *Super Cantica* reveals the special character of his audience: 'To you, brothers, one must discuss different things than are discussed with people in the world, or at least in a different way.'[4] Bernard is correctly associated with incessant and rigorously ascetical cautions against all but the most necessary involvement in the present order. His work is, in fact, an excellent place for ascertaining the evangelical sense of this typical monastic counsel. However, for the non-monk, but total Christian, what does the counsel *not* mean?

That bernardine asceticism which seems to contradict a world-affirming spirituality can be understood and evaluated by placing in the balance against it the *Super Cantica's* concept of contemplation. I would like here to uncover St Bernard's understanding of the relationship of contemplation to action, first, and then to ascetical effort. What character does this contemplative monk give to action on behalf of others and to that christian striving which people inside and outside the tradition came to know, not infrequently to their confusion, as an *-ism*—asceticism?

The action–contemplation dichotomy, with its attendant abstractions, norms, systems, and controversies, has been an intellectual's delight. The further theology moves from religious experience, the more compelling the *quaestio* becomes.

It is human, in an unfortunate sense, to wish to live by formula, to have at any moment in the flux of life a prudence and wisdom assured by precision of doctrine—even when it is known that to be alive to God is not that kind of challenge. The theologian has never been content in his attempts to discern the system that functions in the pages of spiritual writers who assume that Jesus spoke two words to all men and women: 'One thing is needful' (Lk 10:42), and, 'As you did it not to one of the least of these, you did it not to me' (Mt 25:45). It seems important, then, to verify in privileged descriptions of christian experience, like the *Super Cantica,* whether or not the systems which have afforded such intellectual complacence have adequately represented this christian experience. This is one of several reasons I would urge upon the Christian who does not lead the 'contemplative life' to suggest that this is, truly, *his* book or *her* book.

CONTEMPLATION AND ACTION

The reason Bernard perceived great difficulty in combining the activities necessary to human life with contemplation becomes apparent in the statement of his contemplative ambition. He wishes 'not to be bound by the enticements of things in life', nor 'to be wound up in the images of phenomena in thought'.[5] The latter demands a withdrawal from all involvement in human cares. But the abbot is clear about the course to be followed. The 'affective charity' of this contemplation must always give way before the 'active charity' of attention to the needs of one's neighbor.[6] Although this ordering of things is often an affective privation to the devout soul, the author explains its necessity: 'In this lies true charity, that those who have the greater need are served first.'[7] As is frequently the case in Bernard, the depth of the thought—its theological essence—lies in the easily unnoticed scriptural allusion. 'In this lies true charity' (*In hoc est*

caritas, cf. 1 Jn 4:10) implies, but quite clearly and elo-
quently, that the love which is true contemplation is God's
own loving in the soul, and that such love cannot exist in the
soul when she resists its movement toward the needs of
others. Our love for God, 1 Jn 4:10 explains, is God loving in
us 'those who have the greater need' (*qui indigent amplius*),
according to Bernard's gloss; then by the same token, God's
loving another through our *action* can only be resisted at the
cost of a total denaturing of the charity which we presume in
contemplation.

The connection between 1 Jn 4 and the relation of action
and contemplation must be insisted upon. Here is the source
of Bernard's theological conception of the question.[8] Here is
the ultimate source of the cistercian dictum *Amor ipse
intellectus est:* Love itself is the knowing faculty.[9] He who
does not love does not know God, for God is love. From the
clear understanding that activity which meets the needs of
others is the same loving activity of God in the soul as is the
activity of contemplation, Bernard moves on to frequent,
varied, and emphatic expressions of the necessity for the
contemplative of apostolic fraternal charity. Active fraternal
charity, though it disturbs the imagination and drains the
contemplative's strength, is a true act of prayer, an *opus
Dei* (Sermon 50.5).

An effective means of showing the coordinate nature of
action and contemplation is the replacing of the earlier
imagery of the steps or grades of spiritual advance[10] with
such images as the following: Fire that both removes the
superfluous and illumines (57.7); a plant that sends forth
flowers and fruit (47.5); a bush that expands but needs
pruning (58.8); the Bridegroom who is absent but may visit
at any moment (17.1); the beloved who is both spouse and
mother (10.1; 85.13); the anointing of the Head and of the
Body (16.1). the two cheeks of the bride, which are the object and the intention proper to contemplation (40.3); two
sisters, Martha and Mary, who dwell in the same house (51.2);

light in which God may be seen or which may shine before all men (51.2). The most elaborated of these is the image of spouse and mother. In the lyrics of the Song of Songs we encounter lovers. In Bernard's commentary the beloved spouse is also the mother of numerous offspring. In the kiss of contemplation she conceives children whom she must raise (9.7); if her breasts cannot nourish children she is not of marriageable age (10.1); the charms that render her pleasing to the Bridegroom are those which are serviceable to his children (10.1); she must frequently interrupt the pleasure of his kisses in order to nurse their children (4.16; cf. 9.8 and 32.10); the Bridegroom understands her weariness at prayer and loves her for her care to his children (52.6). In his last complete sermon, Bernard wrote: 'The mother rejoices in his offspring, but the spouse rejoices even more in his embrace.'[11]

Just as genuine love must be chaste—in Bernard *castus* means unselfish[12]—so also must contemplation: 'True and chaste [unselfish] contemplation'; 'Most willingly should one interrupt the stillness of contemplation for the effort of preaching.'[13] The reason is that, loving him, the bride wants those he loves also to love him. The abbot set an example of not neglecting his monks in his desire for contemplation (51.3; 52.6; 53.1).

As Bernard spins out endless elaborations of this favorite image, with points of reference ever available in the central image of the Song, it becomes apparent that he has gone beyond the clever manipulation of a usable anthropomorphism. The idea of the love relationship to the Word by which the spouse becomes a mother is the idea of two irreducible dimensions of divine love as it exists in the human subject, as human; and if we add, as a member of the Church, who alone is the spouse, we are not discovering a new facet of the relationship; it is the same facet.

The spouse-mother loves the children of the Bridegroom not occasionally or as an added perfection to her relationship with Him, but out of responsibility; they are hers. Bernard inculcates this attitude toward the neighbor. The cares of life which lay waste contemplative efforts are, in certain contexts, spoken of fondly. The abbot's deceased brother Gerard had been a man who served the community with a responsible feeling. 'How alert in his care!' exclaims Bernard.[14] 'When you put on God, you did not divest yourself of care for us, for even He takes care of us.'[15] That solicitude about necessities which may produce anxiety is spoken of as the wreck of contemplation;[16] but Bernard says of Gerard: 'I was called abbot, but he excelled in solicitude.'[17] Indeed, there is, in the contrast between his gratitude for the *cura* of the lamented Gerard and the usual advice to avoid the cares of material involvements, the suggestion of a rude awakening on the part of an abbot whose burdens of ordinary administration had to some extent been borne by another.

Earlier, Bernard had reminded his contemplative monks, receiving the service of governance from others, that they were 'debtors to the wise and to the foolish.'[18] The storehouse of Scripture, open to the contemplative, contains the wine of discipline by which one is a subject, ointments of nature by which one is a companion, and spices of grace by which one rules. The author explains why grace is claimed preeminently for the exercise of authority: 'Because of the fullness which is received in this alone . . . he who loves his brother has fulfilled the law.'[19] Service, thought the abbot, is one of the marks of the mature soul (9.1-3). Accordingly, he spoke gratefully of the caring office exercised by bishops.[20]

All this puts us in a comfortable position to conclude that when Bernard exhorted his monks to estrange themselves from activity in the world, he was speaking about a special vocation, one that must be legitimated by special religious experience and not by some general assessment of active charity which finds it less urgent or less weighty than any other christian reality.[21]

CONTEMPLATION AND ASCETICISM

To make his integration of action and contemplation more thorough, Bernard joins ascetical effort to action. An early meaning of active life among Greek Christians was the acquiring of virtue (*praktiké*).[22] By adding this to the synthesis, the author makes clear that asceticism is not merely a preparatory phase. One must try to possess this triple good of the soul—Lazarus, Mary and Martha, in one household—'so that one knows how to grieve over himself and, at the same time, to rejoice in God, while maintaining the ability to meet his neighbors' necessities: pleasing to God, cautious toward himself, useful to others.'[23]

Asceticism, then, is related to contemplation the way active charity is. We see this when the author portrays the laborers in the vineyard as ascetics, and says of the fruit of contemplation: 'He who does not labor should not eat.'[24] The ascetic and the apostle share in a common labor, and in its fruit. What is common here is that both strive to prepare for the presence of the Word—the ascetic in his own soul, the apostle in the souls of others.[25]

To evaluate Bernard's asceticism in independence of his contemplative aim is to draw conclusions about an action in ignorance of objective and intention, which constitute the nature of an action. It seems imprudent to dismiss this reflection as obvious. It opens onto a proper understanding of christian asceticism. Friedrich Wulf notes that whereas asceticism may be divided into moral and mystical, 'The traditional Catholic view places the main emphasis on moral asceticism, as a glance at modern ascetic literature will show.'[26] (One must decide, of course, whether texts like Saint Bernard's *Super Cantica* or lesser testimonies should establish 'the traditional Catholic view'.) It is not difficult to demonstrate that Bernard's asceticism is mystical. Admittedly, out of its proper context, it can be easily misread. But if the true sense of his unworldly exhortations is perceived, may one not have new access to their positive content?

Immediately, in the first sermon, a specifically christian character is imparted even to the elementary enterprise of self-control. It is in order to obey the commands of God. The author plans, he says, to treat of the spiritual things of the Song of Songs and must presume that the two preceding books of Solomon, Ecclesiastes and Proverbs, have been mastered (1.2). The reader then is ready, for 'he has placed the fear of God and the observance of his commandments above all human concerns and mundane desires'.[27] He has now a faculty, figuratively speaking, for receiving something beyond the human: 'Competently, now, he may approach this holy contemplative discourse.'[28] Without such a preparation, the reader would be like a blind man upon whose eyes a light was shining (1.3).

The comparison must be noticed. The soul who has not turned from evil and made efforts to obey God's law lacks the very organ of spiritual vision. It is not a question of a greater or lesser degree of ethical rectitude. We read the abbot's sense clearly in his remark: 'The natural man does not perceive what is of the Spirit of God.'[29] Virtues acquired by human effort are not the preparation by which the reader moves on 'competently' to a contemplative discourse. These are signs of co-operation with the Spirit, but the new faculty or capacity is *spiritus* itself, the presence in the soul of the Holy Spirit's activity. The victory, says the abbot to his monks, has been 'your *faith*'.[30] Preparation, in the author's mind, does not refer to a phase of activity which produces skills or good habits, or a measurable moral vigor. The characteristics of the wrong condition may be described— 'The soul burdened with sins and wounded still by the passions of the flesh'[31] —but the right condition, rather than a methodical rise, is a simple turning about, the facing in a new direction, the 'will to repent'.[32]

Bernard does not, even in this introductory discussion about prerequisites, think of ascetical striving merely in a moral sense. Even the elementary moral asceticism of avoiding sin is considered in relation to the heights of contemplation. This establishes the perspective: The renunciations of the soul relate to the vision of God, an anticipation of the final encounter.

Bernard points to this fact in commenting upon the opening words of the Song, 'Oh, that he would kiss me with the kiss of his mouth!'[33] The desire for the divine kiss, he says, is a desire for ultimate contemplative union: 'The touch of lips means the embrace of souls.'[34]

The first theme extensively treated in the *Super Cantica* (throughout the second sermon) is desire, the longing for God. The holy man is the 'man of desire'.[35] Desire which will govern the soul's ascetic striving is directional—up rather than down, in Bernard's language; it establishes a perspective. A frequent consideration for the encouragement of the reader is that, by 'grace's going-before',[36] desire is already a presence of the Word: 'For His desire creates your own.'[37] Bernard's authority for this is the statement that God first loved us (57.6; cf. 1 Jn 4:10). No one forms a desire for the divine kiss from his own desiring, 'out of a natural movement of the soul'[38]; but once he receives the kiss, the experience causes him freely to will its repetition: 'Only he who eats will be hungry.'[39] This love which precedes explains both conversion and growth in virtue: 'It is necessary that He who has given the will to repent add as well the strength to maintain control.'[40] Bernard was too close to Augustine to conceive of virtue as anything but the gift of divine love.[41]

The correlation of asceticism and contemplation as desire and its achievement is expressed in other ways. Contemplation begins in the humility of self-knowledge. This is the key to Bernard's conception of the process.[42] In humility the soul already possesses the Truth. Or, there is the idea that acquiring virtue is a matter of removing the superfluous in order to allow the spirit to grow, 'cutting back the superfluities of the flesh'.[43] 'Remove the superfluous,' he says, 'and the salutary will rise.'[44] An ascetical pruning of the bush is, then, always necessary (58.10). Another way of saying this is that the soul must leave all behind to follow the Word: 'Therefore, when you see a soul that has left all things . . . know it as the spouse, married to the Word.'[45] In each image it is clear that the nature of the ascetical act is established in the contemplative objective.

Expressions of this correlation communicate another aspect of the asceticism of St Bernard: Asceticism and contemplation are a continuum of christian maturing. Asceticism is not viewed merely as that which precedes contemplation; there is love, presence, possession, and seeing, in the ascetical action. Therefore this action is a contemplation. Love is, itself, the knowing-seeing-contemplating faculty, to paraphrase the cistercian dictum (*Amor ipse intellectus est*). Bernard will, of course, speak of the highest *perfection* of love, and of special gifts, as contemplation. But since he encourages all souls to contemplation (62.6; 83.1), it becomes important to understand its continuous character. Consider the following assertions about seeing God: Man must know God from other men, from books, or 'through the things which have been made'.[46] Since not all in the Church can 'penetrate the mysteries of the divine will', to many is given only 'Jesus, and him crucified'.[47] 'For even to have believed is to have seen.'[48] 'The *joy* of hope is already rooted very deeply in the soul.'[49] The contemplative kiss begins with a kiss to the divine feet—conversion (3.2). Clearly the ascetical work which aims to achieve purity of heart is not only a condition of knowledge; it is knowledge.[50]

The relationship of asceticism to love, rather than contemplation, is easier to understand, because love speaks of intent. But for Bernard, in whom contemplation (*intellectus*) is love, the same relationship obtains. One image unites the two—fire, which is the ardor of love and the light of contemplation. Both are present in the asceticism which is thought to precede them; for, says the author, 'Of him you read both that fire precedes him, and that he is, himself, the fire.'[51] The soul which seeks the justice of God in asceticism (57.5) seeks the Word Himself, who is the justice of God (80.2).

The most usual approach to this co-ordinate relationship regards the conformity of the will. We shall see him, says Bernard, and we shall be like him; and it is always clear that this likeness has to do principally with the will. 'We are transformed,' he says, 'when we are conformed.'[52] 'Such a conformity marries the soul to the Word.'[53] As this embrace of marriage is contemplation, so the conformity of the will is the whole of asceticism. Or, as the saint says, 'The embrace, in which the same thing is willed and the same thing not willed, makes one spirit out of two.'[54] To aspire to a common will with God is not a longing for the annihilation of one's humanity, as some have interpreted christian 'mysticism' (read contemplation); it is not a disparagement of the present order.

We come to two conclusions, then, from these considerations of Bernard's notion of contemplation. First, regarding the relation of contemplation to action: Even in that area of his subject where what might be called his spiritualism is given its full scope—Bernard does not want the images of material phenomena to enter his prayer (52.5)!—he shows, by the dignity he accords active fraternal charity, a human solidarity conceived at the highest theological level. The *affective* charity of prayer and the *actual* charity of fraternal care are motions of the same Spirit. Second, with regard to the relation of contemplation to asceticism: Ascetical effort receives its character in its contemplative direction. It is already the love which is contemplation.

If these ideas, precisely as the thought of so classic a medieval monk as Bernard of Clairvaux, did not surprise many today, I would be myself surprised. We do hear much about the obsoleteness of the christian *perfection* ideal, of mystical *withdrawal,* of the *holiness* syndrome, of *scorn* for the world; and we read of their medieval roots. This view

of history may ground so much of one's religious *apologia*
that the prospect of disturbing it may be intolerable. In the
effort to clarify present positions, one tends to arrange
history somewhat, as a foil. But even a minimal ecclesial
sense will produce the saving doubt that perhaps one's past is
not altogether expendable.

Communing with the Christian of yesterday, the Christian
of today comes upon an indispensable heritage. For example, traditionally effort and struggle in the life of Faith has
been reflected upon, profoundly—as in the *Super Cantica.* If
we call this effort asceticism—and perhaps we should, if so
traditional a concept as asceticism is to be legitimated for
the present day—then we are apprised of the wealth of
experience that stands to be lost in facile abandonment of
what is largely unexamined.

The contemporary conviction about the Christian character of working for social justice needs to be enriched with an
earlier age's conception of the linkage between such works
and contemplation and between ascetical effort and contemplation. In St Bernard's text the two relationships are
collapsed into one through the awareness that asceticism and
active charity are simply two manifestations of the divine
love sought in contemplation—one a salutary love of self, the
other a love of the neighbor. It is biblical thought which
makes of both one commandment. If it is the love of self
which must serve as introspective model for the love of
others, one whose love of self is not ascetically wise is something less than a Christ-figure as he goes to encounter the
great suffering world.

Reading Bernard's contemplative book, we find no evidence that the abbot's sense of the scope of God's work in
the non-ecclesiastical world was the same as our sense. But
he knew that the fruit of action was conditioned by the tree
on which it grew. The modern apostle who knew St Bernard
would be alerted against a reliance upon power, against the
protean logic that canonizes the cowardly course, against the

wasted effort of self-seeking, against compassionless ideology, and against the messianism that fails to love the enemy. And, more positively, as he zealously addressed the secular concerns from which Bernard turned away, he would be no more deprived of the Faith-ful awareness of the Christ in need than was Bernard, whose more restricted vision of active charity may have been easier to link with contemplative prayer. The Christian cannot demand that the world see divine love in equitable economics, but he cannot risk losing this vision himself. Anyone who acknowledges that even real progress is not of itself identical with the kingdom of God, and who wishes his struggle for progress to channel God's love to the oppressed and hungry world can turn to the contemplative *Sermones super Cantica Canticorum* to be put in touch with a spring of living water. As he returns to the hungry, he too will know the difference between the leaven and the dough, and between bread and a stone.

EMERO STIEGMAN

Saint Mary's University
Halifax, Nova Scotia.

NOTES

1.   See Jean Leclercq, C. H. Talbot, and H. M. Rochais, eds. *Sermones super cantica canticorum* [SC] I (1957) and II (1958), in *Sancti bernardi Opera,* eds. J. Leclercq and H. M. Rochais (Rome, 1957-   ). The reference here is to SC 1.3: 'Competenter acceditur ad hunc sacrum theoricumque sermonem.' All parenthetical references in the text are to the SC. For other works of St Bernard the Leclercq–Rochais edition is cited as SBOp.

2.   See Robert Bultot, *Christianisme et valeurs humains: La doctrine du mépris du monde en Occident, de S. Ambroise à Innocent II.* Tome iv, *Le XIe siècle:* Vol. 1, *Pièrre Damien* (Louvain, 1963) 39-40. In 'The Theology of Earthly Realities and Lay Spirituality', *Spirituality in the Secular City, Concilium* 19 (New York, 1966) 44-58, at p. 50, n. 11, Bultot makes explicit his opinion that Damian's anthropology is shared by the medieval spiritual writers generally. In 'Spirituels et théologiens devant l'homme et le monde', *Revue Thomiste 64* (Toulouse: Oct.-Dec., 1964) 517-48, at 530-31, the same author examines the thought of St Bernard and includes him in the general censure.

3.   See Ernest Larkin, O. Carm., 'Asceticism in Modern Life' in *Concilium* 19 (New York, 1966) 100-108. Even in this careful and helpful article, one reads (p. 104): 'Detachment rather than charity thus directs the ascetical effort in this [older] system.' The same thought is echoed at p. 108: 'His [i.e., the newer] spiritual life is not structured around the problem of inordinate desires and attachments.' This account does not represent Bernard's thought.

4.   SC 1.1: 'Vobis, fratres, alia quam aliis de saeculo aut certe aliter dicenda sunt.'

5.   SC 52.5: 'Rerum etenim cupiditatibus vivendo non teneri . . . ; corporum vero similitudinibus speculando non involvi.'

6.   SC 50.5 speaks of *caritas affectualis* and *caritas actualis.*

7.   SC 50.6: 'Nam et vera in hoc est caritas, ut qui indigent amplius, accipiant prius.'

8.   Etienne Gilson, *The Mystical Theology of St. Bernard* (New York, 1940) p. 21. The author calls 1 Jn 4 the single most important 'doctrinal bloc' in bernardine thought.

9.   Hans Urs Von Balthasar, *Herrlichkeit: Eine theologischer Ästhetik,* 9 vols. (Einsiedeln, 1961) I:276, remarks: 'The later cistercian theory of love as principle of knowledge, a theory which became so famous, has its source here; and one cannot affirm that it expressed any more than what John says.' (Translation mine.) In Bernard the expression may be found in Div 29, 1; PL 183:620B, as follows: 'Amor ipse est intellectus, notitia est.'

10.   Cf. *De gradibus humilitatis et superbiae,* written before 1124. See SBOp 3:xx, 3, for the dating of the work. The *Sermones super Cantica Canticorum* was written between 1135 and Bernard's death in 1153.

11.   SC 85.13: 'Laeta in prole mater, sed in amplexibus sponsa laetior.'

12.   See, for example, SC 16.4; 78.4; 82.5; and *Dil* XIV, 38; XV, 39, in SBOp 3:152.

13.   SC 57.9: 'Vera et casta contemplatio.' 'Otium contemplationis pro studio praedicationis libentissime intermittat.'

14.   SC 26.4: 'Quam vigil ad curam!'

15.   SC 26.5: 'Nec, quando Deum induisti, nostri cura te exuisti: et ipsi enim cura est de nobis'; cf. 1 P 5:7.

16.   SC 52.4: 'Angores sollicitudinum.'

17.   SC 16.7: 'Ego vocitabar abbas, sed ille praeerat in sollicitudine.'

18.   SC 12.5: 'Sapientibus et insipientibus debitores.'

19.   SC 23.5: 'Ob plenitudinem quae singulariter in ista percipitur . . . . Qui diligit fratrem legem implevit'; cf. Rm 13:8.

20.   See, for example, SC 12.9; 46.2; 77.1; 78.6.

21.   Dom Reginald Grégoire, 'Saeculi actibus se facere alienum: Le "mépris du monde" dans la litterature monastique latine médiévale,' *Revue d'Ascetique et de Mystique* 41 (1965) 251-87, examines St Bernard's understanding of the withdrawal from action and finds it in simple accord with the benedictine tradition and with the *Regula.* The bernardine texts he cites are the *Apologia* 12.28; SBOp 3:105, and the *De diligendo Deo,* 11; SBOp 3:128-29.

22.   See Marcel Viller, *La Spiritualité des premiers siècles chrétiens* (Paris, 1930) p. 59.

23.   SC 57.10: 'Ut et gemere pro se, et exsultare in Deo noverit, simul et proximorum utilitatibus potens sit subvenire: placens Deo, cautus sibi, utilis suis.'

24.   SC 46.5: 'Qui non laborat non manducet'; cf. 2 Th 3:10.

25.   See the same relationship developed at SC 33.8, 15 and SC 77.1.

26.   'Asceticism,' *Sacramentum Mundi* I, 111. Wulf traces the history of the division of asceticism and mysticism into separate theological disciplines, also in modern documents of the Church (p. 114). Two other indices of the existence of a problem among theologians are these: The article of J. De Guibert, et al. 'Ascèse, ascétisme' in DSp, I (1932-37) 930-1010, concludes by noting modern controversies among Catholic theologians over the relation of asceticism to prayer. See 'Ascèse et Prière,' cols. 994-95. Louis Bouyer's preface to the three-volume *Histoire de la spiritualité chrétienne* (Paris, 1966) explains the reason for the work: The current standard work (Paris, 1919-1931) by Pourrat distinguished between ascetical and mystical theology in an unacceptable manner.

27.   SC 1.2: 'Universis humanis studiis ac mundanis desideriis praetulit Deum timere eiusque observare mandata.'

28.   SC 1.3: 'Competenter iam acceditur ad hunc sacrum theoricumque sermonem.'

29.   SC 1.3: 'Ita animalis homo non percipit ea quae sunt Spiritus Dei'; cf. 1 Co 2:14. Bernard's *animalis* is altogether pauline, meaning *of the psycho-physical man*. See, especially the context of 'Prius quod animale deinde quod spirituale', *Dil* VIII, 23; SBOp 3:138-9; cf. 1 Co 15:46.

30.   SC 1.9: 'Fides vestra'; cf. 1 Jn 5:4.

31.   SC 3.1: 'Anima onerata peccatis, suaeque adhuc carnis obnoxia passionibus.'

32.   SC 3.3: 'Voluntas poenitendi.'

33.   SC 1.5; Sg 1.1: 'Osculetur me osculo oris sui.'

34.   SC 2.3: 'Contactus labiorum complexum significat animarum.'

35.   SC 32.2: 'Desiderii vir.'

36.   SC 67.10: 'Gratiae praeventio.'

37.   SC 57.6: 'Illius namque desiderium tuum creat'; cf. 60.1.

38.   SC 3.1: 'Ex affectu.'

39.   SC 3.1 (Si 24:29): 'Solus qui edit adhuc esuriet.' Elsewhere we read: 'Nemo te quaerere valet nisi qui prius invenerit. Vis igitur inveniri ut quaeraris, quaere ut inveniaris.' *Dil* VII, 22; SBOp 3:137-38.

40.   SC 3.3: 'Qui autem dedit voluntatem poenitendi, opus est ut addat et continendi virtutem.'

41.   The pre-eminence of love in the theology of Augustine would

be enough to allow one to assume on traditional grounds, the ordering
of all asceticism under love in St Bernard. Note Augustine's definition of
virtue as 'the order of love' (*ordo amoris*), *De civitate dei*, 15.22; PL 41:
467. See A. Wilmart, 'L'Ancienne Bibliothèque de Clairvaux,' *Memoires
de la Société académique...du Department de l'Aube* 81 (1917), 125-90;
reproduced in part in *Collectanea o.c.r.* 11 (1949) 101-27, 301-19—on
Augustine, pp. 108-117. Studying a 1472 inventory of the twelfth-
century Clairvaux library, Dom Wilmart noted that the great number
of MSS were of the works of Augustine; and that these were listed
first, after the Bible, before the catalog proceeded with its chrono-
logical order. This was because Augustine was 'the traditional doctrine
in the eyes of a monk of the twelfth century'. See Jean Leclercq,
'Les Mss de l'abbaye de Liessies,' *Scriptorium* 6 (1952) 51-53.
Leclercq shows that six of the seven volumes of the Liessies monastery
holdings on Augustine—that is, those mentioned by Dom Wilmart,
above—are 'St Bernard's personally made copies' (p. 53). A reasonable
working hypothesis for the examination of major spiritual writers in
'the Catholic tradition' up to the seventeenth century is that their
asceticism has the theoretical love-orientation which we are here discovering in Bernard.

42.   See, for example, SC 23.17; 46.5. A good résumé is J. M. Dé-
chanet, 'Contemplation,' D Sp II, cols. 1949-50.

43.   SC 1.2: 'Carnis superflua resecans.' In St Bernard, 'the flesh',
caro, has the pauline meaning (Ga 5:16-26; Rm 8:1-13) of creaturely
humanity, not of the *body*. See SC 1.9; 20.4; 20.7; 26.9; 31.6; 38.4;
56.2; 66.7; 81.4; 81.10; 85.4; etc. Some passages may seem to create
difficulties (for example, SC 7.3; 29.7; and 50.4), but upon careful
contextual reading they are found to be expressions of St Paul's
flesh-and-spirit contrast.

44.   SC 58.10: 'Tolle superflua, et salubria surgunt.'

45.   SC 85.12: 'Ergo, quam videris animam, relictis omnibus . . .
puta coniugem, Verboque maritatam'; cf. Lk 5:11. On this text Kurt
Knotzinger, 'Hoheslied und bräutliche Christusliebe bei Bernhard von
Clairvaux,' *Jahrbuch für mystische Theologie* 7 (1961) 7-88, at p. 86,
says, 'With this, in brief, the ascetical presupposition [*Voraussetzung*]
for the mystical encounter is named' [my translation]. But, is not
more named here than a presupposition?

46.   SC 53.5: 'Per ea quae facta sunt': cf. Rm 1:20.

47.   SC 62.6: 'Sacramenta divinae voluntatis inspicere.' 'Jesum et
hunc crucifixum'; cf. 1 Co 2:2. The author varies this imagery pro-
fusely in this passage, to assure the timid. 'Not in all its parts,' he says,
'can the Church approach the rock to penetrate it (*Non ex omni se*

interim parte adhuc ad petram forandam accedere Ecclesia potest).'
Some, like the dove of the Song of Songs, will nestle into the clefts of
the rock or in the covert of the cliff (Sg 2:14).

48.   SC 70.2: 'Et credidisse enim, vidisse est.'

49.   SC 37.5: 'Laetitiaque spei iam altius radicata in animo.'

50.   See M. P. Delfgaauw, 'La Lumière de la charité chez saint
Bernhard,' *Collectanea o.c.r.* 18 (1956) 42-67, 306-20, at p. 319.

51.   SC 57.7: 'Etenim utrumque de illo legis, et ignem videlicet
ante ipsum praecedere et ipsum nihilominus ignem esse'; cf. Ps 96:3
(Vulg.), and Dt 4:24.

52.   SC 62.5: 'Transformamur cum conformamur.'

53.   SC 83.3: 'Tallis conformitas maritat animam Verbo.'

54.   SC 83.3: 'Complexus plane, ubi idem velle, et nolle idem,
unum facit spiritum de duobos'; cf. 1 Co 6:17.

BERNARD OF CLAIRVAUX

ON THE SONG OF SONGS, III

SERMON FORTY-SEVEN

I. THE FLOWER OF THE FIELD, OF THE
GARDEN AND OF THE BRIDAL SUITE.
II. A FURTHER INTERPRETATION, AND
WHY HE SPECIFICALLY CALLS HIMSELF
THE FLOWER OF THE FIELD. III. WHY
HE CALLS HIMSELF THE LILY OF THE
VALLEY, AND HOW EAGER WE OUGHT
TO BE FOR THE WORK OF GOD.

I. 1. 'I AM THE FLOWER of the field and the lily of the valleys'.* I feel that these words refer to the bride's commendation of the bed for its adornment with flowers. For lest she should commend herself for these flowers, with which the bed was bedecked and the room made beautiful, the Bridegroom states that he is the flower of the field, that the flowers were a product of the field, not of the room. Their splendor and perfume result from his favor and contribution. Lest anyone should reproach her and say: 'What do you have that you did not receive? If you received it, then why do you

*Sg 2:1

3

*1 Cor 4:7
boast as if it were not a gift?'* he, a concerned lover and kindly teacher, lovingly and
courteously tells his beloved who it is to
whom she should ascribe the splendor of
which she boasted and the sweet perfume of
the bed. 'I am the flower of the field,' he said:
it is of me that you boast. We are well advised
*2 Cor 12:1
from this that one ought never to boast,* and
if one does boast he should boast of the
*1 Cor 1:31
Lord.* So much for the literal meaning; let us
now with the help of him of whom we speak,
examine the spiritual meaning that it conceals.

2. To begin, I now take note of the three
places in which a flower is found: in the field,
in the garden, in the room, that we may
afterwards more easily ascertain why he
especially chooses to be called the flower of
the field. A flower grows both in field and
garden, but in a room never. It brightens and
perfumes it, not by standing upright as in the
garden or field, but by lying prone because it
is brought from without, not sprung from
within. So it is they must be frequently
renewed, fresher blooms must always be
added, because they soon lose their scent
and beauty. And if, as I have stated in another
sermon, the bed bedecked with flowers is the
conscience laden with good works, you must
certainly see that it is by no means enough to
do a good deed once or twice if the likeness is
to be preserved; you must unceasingly add
new ones to the former, so that sowing
*2 Cor 9:6
bountifully you may reap bountifully.* Otherwise the flower of good works withers where
it lies, and all its brilliance and freshness are
swiftly destroyed if it is not renewed con-

tinually by more and more acts of love. So it is in the room.

3. In the garden however it is not so; nor is it in the field, for of themselves they constantly nourish the blooms they produce, which, in consequence, retain their native beauty. Yet there is this difference, that the garden flourishes because it is cultivated by the hand and skill of men, but the field produces flowers naturally of itself, without the aid of human labor. Do you think you now perceive who that field is: it is not furrowed by the plow, nor broken with the hoe, nor fertilized with dung, nor sown by the hand of man, but nevertheless made honorable by that noble flower on which the Spirit of the Lord has clearly rested?* 'See, my son's scent is as the scent of a field which the Lord has blessed'.* That flower of the field had not as yet put on its beauty and already it produced its fragrance,* when the holy and aged patriarch, with enfeebled body and failing sight but a keen sense of smell, pre-sensed it in spirit and uttered those joyful words. He who is the flower in perpetual bloom could not therefore proclaim himself a flower of the room, nor yet of the garden, lest he seem begotten by human means. But he who was born without human effort said in a way both beautiful and becoming: 'I am the flower of the field.' And once born he was never thereafter subjected to corruption, that the word might be fulfilled which says: 'You will not allow your holy one to see corruption.'*

Is 11:2

Gen 27:27

Sg 1:11

Ps 15:10 (Vulgate)

II. 4. But listen, if you please, to another explanation of this problem, in my opinion not to be slighted. It is not without reason that the spirit is called manifold by the Wise Man,* if only because it usually contains different meanings under the text's one shell. Therefore, in accord with the aforesaid distinction concerning the flower's situation, the flower is virginity, it is martyrdom, it is good work: in the garden, virginity; in the field, martyrdom; in the room, good work. And how suitable the garden is for virginity that has modesty for companion, that shuns publicity, is happy in retirement, patient under discipline. The flower is enclosed in the garden, exposed in the field, strewn about in the room. You have 'a garden enclosed, a fountain sealed'.* In the virgin it seals up the doorway of chastity, the safeguard of untainted holiness, provided however that she is one who is holy both in body and spirit.* Suitable the field too for martyrdom, for the martyrs are exposed to the ridicule of all, made a spectacle to angels and to men.* Is not theirs the pitiful voice of the psalm: 'We have become a taunt to our neighbors, mocked and derided by those round about us?'* Suitable, too, is the room for good works that foster a safe and quiet conscience. After a good work one rests more securely in contemplation, and the more a man is conscious that he has not failed in works of charity through love of his own ease, the more faithfully will he contemplate things sublime and make bold to study them.

5. And all these, in each way, mean the Lord Jesus. He is the flower of the garden,

*Wis 7:22

*Sg 4:12

*1 Cor 7:34

*1 Cor 4:9

*Ps 78:4

a virgin shoot sprung from a virgin. He is the
flower of the field, martyr and crown of
martyrs, the exemplar of martyrdom. For he
was led outside the city, he suffered 'outside
the camp',* he was raised on the cross to be   *Heb 13:12-13*
stared by all, to be mocked by all.* He is   *Jer 20:7, Ps 21:8*
also the flower of the room, the mirror and
the model of all helpfulness, as he himself
testified to the Jews: 'I have done many good
works among you',* and Scripture says of   *Jn 10:32*
him: 'he went about doing good and healing
all'.* If the Lord then is all three of these, *Acts 10:38*
what was the reason that of the three he preferred to be called 'flower of the field'?
Surely so that he might inspire in her* the   *the Church of
endurance to suffer the persecution that he   Sermon 46.*
knew was imminent if she wished to live a
godly life in Christ.* Hence he eagerly pro-   *2 Tim 3:12*
claims himself to be that for which he
especially wishes to have a following; and
that is what I have said elsewhere: she always
longs for quietness and he arouses her to
labor, impressing on her that through many
tribulations we must enter the kingdom of
heaven.* When he had arranged to return to   *Acts 14:21*
the Father, then, he said to the young Church
on earth which he had recently betrothed to
himself: 'The hour comes when whoever kills
you will think he is offering service to God;'* *Jn 16:2*
and again: 'If they persecuted me they will
persecute you'.* You too can gather many   *Jn 15:20*
texts in the Gospels similar to this proclamation of evils to be endured.

6. 'I am the flower of the field and the
lily of the valley.'* While she therefore draws *Sg 2:1*
attention to the bed, he summons her to the

field, he challenges to exertion. Nor does he consider any motivation for undertaking the contest more compelling for her than to propose himself as the exemplar or reward of the contender. 'I am the flower of the field.' In fact, the words may be understood in either of these two senses: the form of combat or the glory of the victor. To me, Lord Jesus, you are both, both the mirror of endurance and the reward of the sufferer. Both are a strong challenge, a vehement incitement. By the example of your virtue you train my hands for war;* by your regal presence you crown my head in victory. Whether I see you doing battle, or whether I look to you not only as the crowner but the crown as well, in both you attract me wonderfully to yourself. Each is a powerful cord to draw me on.* 'Draw me after you',* willingly do I follow, and still more willingly enjoy it. If you are so good, O Lord, to those who follow you, what will you be to those who overtake you? 'I am the flower of the field': let him who loves me come into the field, let him not refuse to undertake the struggle, with me and for me, that he may be enabled to say: 'I have fought the good fight.'*

Ps 17:35

Hos 11:4
Sg 1:3

2 Tim 4:7

III. 7.   And since it is not the proud or the arrogant, but rather the humble, who know nothing of self-reliance, that are fit for martyrdom, he adds that he is 'the lily of the valley', that is, the reward of the humble, designating by the excellence of this flower the special glory of their future exaltation. For a time shall come when every valley shall

be filled and every mountain and hill be made
low,* and then he, the brightness of eternal   *Is 40:4*
life,* will appear as the lily, not of the hills   *Wis 7:26*
but of the valleys. 'The just man shall blossom
as the lily,'* says the prophet. Who is just if   *Hos 14:6*
not the humble man? In short, when the Lord
bowed down under the hands of his servant
the Baptist, who recoiled in fear of his
majesty, he said: 'Let it be; it is fitting that
we should in this way do all that righteous-
ness demands',* thereby assigning the fulness   *Mt 3:15*
of righteousness to perfect humility. The just
man therefore is humble, the just man is a
valley. And if we shall have been found to be
humble, we too shall blossom as the lily, and
bloom for ever before the Lord. Will he not
truly and in a special way reveal himself as a
lily of the valley when 'he will transfigure
these wretched bodies of ours into copies of
his glorious body'?* He does not say 'our   *Phil 3:21*
body' but 'our wretched bodies', to indicate
that the humble alone would be enlightened
by the marvellous and eternal brightness of
this lily. These things have been said because
of the Bridegroom's declaration that he is the
flower of the field and the lily of the valley.

8.   At this point it would be good to hear
what he will say of his dearly beloved; but the
time does not permit. By our Rule we must
put nothing before the work of God.* This is   *RB 43:2*
the title by which our Father Benedict chose
to name the solemn praises that are daily
offered to God in the oratory, that so he
might more clearly reveal how attentive he
wanted us to be at that work. So, dearest
brothers, I exhort you to participate always

in the divine praises correctly and vigorously: vigorously, that you may stand before God with as much zest as reverence, not sluggish, not drowsy, not yawning, not sparing your voices, not leaving words half-said or skipping them, not wheezing through the nose with an effeminate stammering, in a weak and broken tone, but pronouncing the words of the Holy Spirit with becoming manliness and resonance and affection; and correctly, that while you chant you ponder on nothing but what you chant. Nor do I mean that only vain and useless thoughts are to be avoided; but, for at least that time and in that place, those also must be avoided with which office-holders must be inevitably and frequently preoccupied for the community's needs. Nor would I even recommend that you dwell on those you have just freshly acquired as you sat in the cloisters reading books, or such as you are now gathering from the Holy Spirit during my discussions in this lecture-hall. They are wholesome, but it is not wholesome for you to ponder them in the midst of the psalms. For if at that time you neglect what you owe, the Holy Spirit is not pleased to accept anything offered that is not what you owe. May we always be able to do his will in accord with *Ps 142:10*   his will,* as he inspires, by the grace and mercy of the Church's Bridegroom, our Lord *Rom 1:25*   Jesus Christ, who is blessed for ever.* Amen.

SERMON FORTY-EIGHT

1. AS A LILY AMONG THORNS, SO THE
SOUL AMID SINS.   II. A EULOGY IN
WHICH THE BRIDEGROOM IS COMPARED
TO AN APPLE-TREE AMID THE TREES
OF THE WOOD, AND WHAT IT MEANS
TO BE PRAISED BY THE BRIDEGROOM
OR TO PRAISE HIM.   III. CONCERNING
THE SHADOW OF THE BELOVED, AND
THE FAITH AND CONTEMPLATION THAT
ARE ITS SWEET FRUIT.

I. 1. 'AS A LILY AMONG THORNS so is my love among maidens.'* Maidens who are vexing are not good. Consider the evil produce of this curse-laden earth of ours. 'When you till it,' he said, 'it will grow thorns and thistles for you.'* Therefore while the soul is in the flesh it dwells among thorns and suffers of necessity the disquietude of temptations, the pangs of tribulation. And if, according to the Bridegroom's word, she is a lily, let her consider how vigilant and careful she should be in guarding herself, hedged all around with thorns whose sharp points threaten her on every side. For the tender flower cannot resist even the lightest prick of the thorn, it is no sooner prodded than pierced. Do you not see how rightly and

*Sg 2:2

*Gen 3:18

11

*Ps 2:11
*Phil 2:12

unavoidably the prophet exhorts us to serve the Lord with fear,* and the apostle to work out our salvation with fear and trembling?* For they learned by their own experience the truth of this observation, and as friends of the Bridegroom they would never hesitate to apply to themselves the words: 'As a lily among thorns so is my love among maidens.'

*Ps 31:4

Or as one of them said: 'I am turned in my anguish while the thorn is fastened'.* Well pierced is the one who is thereby converted. You are well wounded if you repent. Many, when they feel the pain, correct the fault. Such a one can say: 'I am turned in my

*Ibid.

anguish while the thorn is fastened.'* The thorn is the fault, the thorn is the pain, the thorn is the false brother, the thorn is the bad neighbor.

2. 'As a lily among thorns so is my love among maidens.' O shining lily! Tender and delicate flower! Unbelieving and seditious men surround you: see that you tread with

*Ezek 2:6,
  Eph 5:15

care among the thorns.* The world is full of thorns. They are in the earth, in the air, in your flesh. To live among them and not be harmed is the fruit of God's power, not of your virtue. But he said: 'Have confidence,

*Jn 16:33

for I have overcome the world.'* Therefore although you foresee trials that menace you like thorns or thistles, let not your heart be

*Jn 14:1

afraid,* knowing that suffering produces endurance, and endurance produces character, and character produces hope, and hope does

*Rom 5:3-5

not disappoint us'.* Consider the lilies of the field, how they thrive and bloom amid the

*Mt 6:28

thorns.* If God cares so much for the grass

that today is alive and tomorrow is cast into the oven, how much more will he care for his beloved and dearest bride?* In short, 'the Lord preserves all who love him'.* 'As a lily among thorns so is my love among maidens.' It is no small proof of virtue to live a good life among the wicked, to retain the glow of innocence and gentleness of manners among the malicious; above all to show that you are peaceful with those who hate peace and a friend to your very enemies.* That will clearly lay your claim in a special way, with a certain proprietary right, to the likeness of the lily, which does not cease to embellish and beautify with its own brightness the very thorns that pierce it. And in this way does the lily not seem to you somehow to achieve the perfection of the Gospel, by which we are commanded to pray for our calumniators and persecutors, to do good to those who hate us?* Do likewise,† therefore, and your soul will be the Lord's own friend and he will praise you for what you are, saying that 'as a lily among thorns so is my love among maidens'.

II. 3. She continues: 'As an apple-tree among the trees of the wood, so is my beloved among the sons.'* The bride returns the compliment of praise addressed to her by the Bridegroom; to be praised by him is to be made worthy of praise, and to praise him is to understand and wonder at his excellence. And just as the Bridegroom's praise of her was symbolized by the beautiful flower, so she for her part typifies his unique glory and excel-

*Mt 6:30
*Ps 144:20

*Ps 119:7

*Mt 5:44
†Lk 10:37

*Sg 2:3

lence by a noble tree. And yet I have an impression about this tree that its excellence does not appear as great as that of some others, and that therefore it has been inappropriately adopted as an object of comparison, since it is inadequate to fulfil the role of praise. 'As an apple tree among the trees of the wood, so is my beloved among the sons.' Indeed the bride herself does not seem to rate it highly, since she takes care to extol it only among the trees of the wood, sterile trees that bear no fruit suitable for human food. Why, when the finer and nobler trees were ignored, was the insignificance of this tree brought forward to eulogize the Bridegroom? Should he thus receive praise by measure who has not received the Spirit by measure?* For to compare him with that tree seems to indicate that he who has no equal has a superior. What shall we say to this?* I say the praise is little because it is praise from one who is little. Because in this place the announcement is not: 'Great is the Lord and greatly to be praised,'* but, little is the Lord and greatly to be loved: the child namely, who is born to us.*

4. Majesty, therefore, is not being exalted here, but humility worthily and reasonably commended, because the weakness and foolishness of God is preferred to the strength and wisdom of men.* These are the fruitless woodland trees, for according to the prophet: 'they have all gone astray, they are all alike corrupt; there is none that does good, no, not one.'* 'As an apple tree among the trees of the wood, so is my beloved among the

*Jn 3:34

*Rom 8:31

*Ps 47:2

*Is 9:6

*1 Cor 1:25

*Ps 13:3

sons.' Alone among the trees of the wood the
Lord Jesus is the tree that bears fruit,* as a *Lk 3:9*
man although more perfect than men, yet
lower than the angels.* In a wonderful way *Heb 2:9*
he both subjected himself as man to the
angels and, remaining God, retained the angels
as his subjects. As he said: 'You will see the
angels ascending and descending upon the
Son of Man,'* since in one and the same *Jn 1:51*
Christ Jesus they both support his weakness
and gaze in awe at his majesty. Since therefore
his littleness gives sweeter relish to the bride,
she more willingly extols his grace, proclaims
his mercy, is lost in wonder at his kindness.
She has been happy to contemplate him as a
man among men, not as God among the
angels: just as an apple tree is superior among
the trees of the wood and not obviously
among the plants of the garden. Nor does she
consider that his praises are diminished when
his loving goodness is lauded in terms of his
frailty. And if, from one viewpoint, she
moderates her praise, from another she praises
all the more, dilating less on the glory of his
excellence in order that the grace of his kindness may stand revealed. Just as the apostle,
therefore, says that the foolishness and weakness of God is wiser and stronger than men,* *1 Cor 1:25*
but not than angels, and as the prophet
proclaims him the fairest of the sons of
men,* and not of angels, so she, speaking *Ps 44:3*
certainly in the same Spirit,* wished to make *1 Cor 12:3*
known here, under the image of the fruitful
tree amid the woodland trees, that God made
man surpasses all human greatness, but not
the excellence of the angelic nature.

5. 'As an apple tree among the trees of the wood, so is my beloved among the sons.' And fittingly 'among the sons', because although he was the only Son of his Father, he made it his aim to acquire for him without envy many sons whom he is not ashamed to call brothers,* that he might be the first-born among many brothers.* But he who is son by nature is rightly preferred to all those adopted by grace. 'As an apple tree among the trees of the wood so is my beloved among the sons.' Justly 'as an apple tree', since after the manner of a fruit-bearing tree he casts a refreshing shadow and yields excellent fruit. Is that not truly a fruit-bearing tree whose flowers are the fruit of honor and uprightness?* In short 'he is the tree of life to those who lay hold of him'.* All the trees of the wood shall not be compared to him, because although they are trees, great and beautiful trees which seem to provide help by praying, ministering, teaching, assisting by good example, Christ alone, the Wisdom of God,* is the tree of life,† he alone the living bread which comes down from heaven* and gives life to the world.

III. 6. Therefore she says: 'In his shadow, for which I longed, I am seated, and his fruit is sweet to my taste.'* Justly did she long for the shadow of the one from whom she would receive both refreshment and nourishment. For the other trees of the wood may indeed provide a comforting shadow, but not a life-giving food, not the enduring fruits of salvation. There is only one 'author of life',*

*Heb 2:11
*Rom 8:29

*Sir 24:23
*Prov 3:18

*1 Cor 1:24
†Gen 2:9
*Jn 6:51

*Sg 2:3

*Acts 3:5

'one mediator between God and men, the man Christ Jesus',* who says to his bride: 'I am your deliverance'.* 'It was not Moses,' he said, 'who gave you the bread from heaven; my Father gives you the true bread from heaven.'* Consequently she longed most specially for the shadow of Christ, because he alone would not only refresh her from the fever-heat of vices, but would fill her too with delight in the virtues. 'In his longed-for shadow I am seated.' His shadow is his flesh; his shadow is faith. The flesh of her own Son overshadowed Mary; faith in the Lord overshadows me. And yet why should his flesh not overshadow me too, as I eat him in the sacrament? And even the holy Virgin herself experienced the shadow of faith, for to her was said: 'Blessed are you who believed.'* 'In his longed-for shadow I am seated.' The prophet says: 'A spirit before our face is Christ the Lord, in his shadow we live among the pagans.'* In the shadow among the pagans, in the light with the angels. We are in the shadow as long as we walk by faith and not by sight;* and therefore the righteous man who lives by faith is in the shadow.* But happy is he who lives by his understanding, because he is no longer in the shadow but in the light. David was a righteous man and lived by faith, for he said to God: 'Give me understanding and I shall live',* knowing that understanding would follow on faith, that the light of life* would be revealed to the understanding, and life to light. The first thing is to come to the shadow, and then to pass on to that of which it is the shadow, because he

*1 Tim 2:5
*Ps 34:3

*Jn 6:32

*Lk 1:45

*Lam 4:20 (LXX)

*2 Cor 5:7
*Rom 1:17

*Ps 118:144

*Jn 8:12

says: 'Unless you believe you will not understand.'*

Is 7:9 (LXX)

7. You see that faith is both life and the
shadow of life. On the other hand, a life
spent amid pleasures, since it is not by faith,
is both death and the shadow of death. 'A
widow given over to self-indulgence', says
the apostle, 'is dead even while she lives.'*
'To set the mind on the flesh is death.'* It is
also the shadow of death, of that death which
torments into eternity. We too once sat in
darkness and the shadow of death,* following
the way of the flesh and not living by faith,*
already indeed dead to righteousness* and on
the point of being swallowed up by the second
death.* For as close as the shadow is to the
body of which it is the shadow, so close, for
sure, did our life come near hell.* Then, 'if
the Lord had not been my help, my soul
would soon have dwelt in hell.'* Now however we have passed from the shadow of
death to the shadow of life, or rather we have
passed from death to life* and live in the
shadow of Christ, provided we are alive and
not dead. Nor do I imagine that everyone
who is in his shadow lives in it, because
obviously not everyone who has the faith
lives by faith. Now 'faith apart from works is
dead,'* it cannot impart a life of which it is
totally devoid. Therefore when the prophet
said: 'A spirit before our face is Christ the
Lord', he was not content to go on and say,
'we are in his shadow', but: 'in his shadow we
live among the pagans'. Be careful therefore
that you live in his shadow as the prophet
did, so that one day you may reign in his

1 Tim 5:6
Rom 8:6

Lk 1:79
Rom 1:17
1 Pet 2:24

Rev 20:6

Ps 87:4

Ps 93:17

1 Jn 3:14

Jas 2:20

light. For he not only possesses a shadow, he also has light. Through his flesh he is the shadow of faith, through his spirit he is the light of the mind. He is flesh and he is spirit. He is flesh to those who remain in the flesh, but 'a spirit before our face', that is, in the future, provided we forget what lies behind and strain forward to what lies ahead,* where on arriving we may experience exactly what he said: 'The flesh is of no avail; it is the spirit that gives life.'* Nor am I unaware that the apostle while still living in the flesh said: 'Even if we did once know Christ in the flesh, that is not how we know him now'.* But this was his privilege. We, however, who have not yet merited to be rapt into paradise, into the third heaven,* let us meanwhile be fed with the flesh of Christ, let us honor his mysteries, follow his footsteps, preserve the faith, and we will certainly be living in his shadow.

*Phil 3:13

*Jn 6:63

*2 Cor 5:16

*2 Cor 12:4,2

8. 'In his longed-for shadow I am seated.' Perhaps she is priding herself on having had a happier experience in that, unlike the prophet, she says she does not live, but is seated, in his shadow. To be seated is to be at ease. It is a greater thing to be at ease in the shadow than to live there, just as to live is greater than merely to be there. The prophet therefore takes what is common to many and says: 'in his shadow we live';* the bride however, enjoying a privilege, boasts that she alone is seated beneath it. Not as he said in the plural, 'we live', did she say, 'we are seated', but in the singular 'I am seated', that you may recognize the privilege. Where we toil as we live, we who, aware of our sins, serve with fear, there

*Lam 4:20

*1 Jn 4:18

*1 Cor 13:12

*Sg 2:17, 4:6

*Rom 9:5

she, in loving commitment, is sweetly at rest. In short, fear awaits punishment,* love delight. Hence she says: 'And his fruit is sweet to my taste', suggesting the taste of him she received in contemplation when sweetly inspired by love. But that was in shadow, because 'in a mirror and in a riddle'.* A time will come however when the shadows will wane and even entirely fade away with the advance of dawn,* and a vision as clear as it is everlasting will steal upon her, bringing not only sweetness to her taste but fulfilment to her heart, yet without surfeit: 'In his longed-for shadow I am seated, and his fruit is sweet to my taste.' Where the bride rests let us also rest, giving praise for the portion received to the Head of the family who invited us to such a banquet, to the Church's Bridegroom, Jesus Christ our Lord, who is over all things, God, blessed for ever.* Amen.

SERMON FORTY-NINE

1. THE WINE CELLAR: THIS INDICATES THE EARLY CHURCH, OR A ZEAL FOR RIGHTEOUSNESS THAT BURNS IN THE SOUL FROM CONTEMPLATING GOD. II. THE DISCIPLINE OF LOVE IS DISCRETION. III. PROJECTS THAT COME UP FOR DECISION MUST SOMETIMES BE POSTPONED FOR THE SAKE OF ORDERLY LOVE, AND THAT WE SHOULD BE ALL THE MORE HAPPY BECAUSE OF THE GREATER GAIN TO GOD. IV. HOW WE MAY ATTAIN TO THE RIGHT ORDER OF LOVE.

I. 1. 'THE KING LED ME into the wine-cellar, he set love in order in me.'* The words of the proposed *Sg 2:3 text seem to mean that after the bride had achieved her desire of sweet and intimate conversation with her beloved, she returned, at his departure, to the maidens so refreshed and animated in speech and appearance that she looked drunken. And when they, surprised at this novelty, asked for the reason, she answered that it is not surprising if one who entered the wine-cellar should be tipsy with wine. So much for the literal meaning.

21

But she also does not deny that she is drunk
in the spirit, but with love, not wine—except
that love is wine. 'The king led me into the
wine-cellar.' When the bridegroom is present
and the bride addresses him, then 'bridegroom' is said, or 'beloved' or 'whom my soul
loves'; but when she speaks about him to the
maidens she calls him 'the king'. Why? Because it is appropriate for the bride who loves
and is loved to use familiarly, as she pleases,
the titles of love, and it is necessary that the
maidens, who need discipline, be constrained
by the awesome title of majesty.

2. 'The king led me into the wine-cellar.'
I omit mentioning what that wine-cellar is,
because I remember having described it.*
But if the term is referred to the Church—
since the disciples, filled with the Holy Spirit,
were thought by the people to be drunk with
wine*—then Peter, the friend of the bridegroom,* standing in their midst said on behalf
of the bride: 'These men are not drunk as
you suppose.'* Take note that he denies not
that they are drunk, but drunk in the manner
supposed by the people. For they were drunk,
but with the Holy Spirit, not with wine. And
as if they would witness to the people that
they had really been led into the wine-cellar,
again Peter says on behalf of all:* 'But this is
what was spoken by the prophet Joel: "and
in the last days it shall be, God declares, that
I will pour out my Spirit upon all flesh, and
your sons and your daughters shall prophesy,
and your young men shall see visions, and your
old men shall dream dreams".'* Does it not
seem to you that the wine-cellar was that

*Serm 23, 5
(CF 7:29)

*Acts 2:4-13

*Jn 3:29

*Acts 2:15

*Acts 2:16-17

*Joel 2:28

house in which the disciples were assembled,*   **Jn 20:19*
when 'suddenly a sound came from heaven
like the rush of a mighty wind, and it filled all
the house where they were sitting,'* and   **Acts 2:2*
fulfilled Joel's prophecy? And as each of
them went out intoxicated by the abundance
of that house* and drunk from a torrent of   **Ps 35:9*
a pleasure so great, could he not truly say:
'the king led me into the wine-cellar'?

3. But even you too, if recollected in
spirit, if with a mind serious and devoid of
cares, you enter the house of prayer* alone,   **Mt 21:13*
and standing in the Lord's presence at one of
the altars touch the gate of heaven with the
hand of holy desire, if in the presence of the
choirs of saints where your devotion penetrates—for 'the prayer of the righteous man
pierces the heavens'*—you bewail pitiably   **Sir 35:21*
before them the miseries and misfortunes
you endure, manifest your neediness, im-
plore their mercy with repeated sighs and
groanings too deep for words; if, I say, you
do this, I have confidence in him who said:
'ask and you shall receive,'* that if you con-   **Jn 16:24*
tinue knocking you will not go empty away.*   **Lk 11:8*
Indeed when you return to us full of grace
and love, you will not be able, in the ardor of
your spirit,* to conceal the gift you have   **Rom 12:11*
received; you will communicate it without
unpopularity,* and in the grace that was   **Wis 7:13*
given to you, you will win the acceptance
and even the admiration of everyone. And
you can declare with truth: 'the king led me
into the wine-cellar'; only be careful that you
glory not in yourself but in the Lord.* I   **1 Cor 1:31*
would not vouch that every gift, even if

spiritual, proceeds from the wine-cellar, since
the bridegroom has other cellars or reposi-
tories in which are hidden varying gifts and
charisms, in accord with the riches of his
glory.* I have discoursed on these cellars
quite extensively elsewhere.* 'Are these not
laid up in store with me,' he said, 'sealed up
in my treasuries?'* Therefore there is a distri-
bution of graces* in accord with the diversity
of cellars, and 'to each is given the manifestation of the Spirit for the common good'. And
although one is given wisdom in speech, another the power to instruct, another prophecy, another the grace of healing, another
the gift of tongues, another the ability to
interpret doctrine,* and still others gifts
similar to these, yet none of them can say in
consequence that he was led into the wine-
cellar. For these are taken from other cellars
or treasuries.

4. But if anyone obtains, while praying,
the grace of going forth in spirit into the
mystery of God,* and then returns in a glowing ardor of divine love, overflowing with
zeal for righteousness, fervent beyond measure in all spiritual studies and duties, so that
he can say: 'My heart became hot within me;
as I mused the fire burned',* since the abundance of love shows he has clearly begun to
live in that state of good and salutary intoxication, he is not unjustly said to have entered
the wine-cellar. For as holy contemplation
has two forms of ecstasy, one in the intellect,
the other in the will; one of enlightenment,
the other of fervor; one of knowledge, the
other of devotion: so a tender affection, a

Eph 3:16

*Serm 23, 5-8
(CF 7:29-33)*

Deut 32:34

1 Cor 12:14

1 Cor 12:7-10

2 Cor 5:13

Ps 38:4

heart glowing with love, the infusion of holy ardor, and the vigor of a spirit filled with zeal, are obviously not acquired from any place other than the wine-cellar. And everyone to whom it is granted to rise up from prayer with an abundance of these can truly say: 'the king led me into the wine-cellar.'

II. 5. She continues: 'He set love in order in me'.* Utterly necessary. Zeal without knowledge is insupportable.* Therefore where zeal is enthusiastic, there discretion, that moderator of love, is especially necessary. Because zeal without knowledge always lacks efficacy, is wanting in usefulness, and all too often is harmful. And so the more eager the zeal, the more vigorous the spirit, the more generous the love, so also the greater the need for more vigilant knowledge to restrain the zeal, to temper the spirit, to moderate the love. Hence the bride, lest she be feared by the maidens as overbearing and insufferable because of the impetuosity of spirit that she seems to have brought back from the wine-cellar, adds that she too has received the fruit of discretion, a regulating of love. Discretion regulates every virtue, order assigns proportion and beauty, and even permanence. For it is written: 'By your ordinance the day goes on',* day meaning virtue. Discretion therefore is not so much a virtue as a moderator and guide of the virtues, a director of the affections, a teacher of right living. Take it away and virtue becomes vice, and natural affection itself a force that disturbs and destroys nature. 'He set love in order in me.'

*Sg 2:4
*Rom 10:2

*Ps 118:91

Eph 4:11

This took place when he appointed some in
the Church to be apostles, some prophets,
others evangelists, others pastors and teachers,
for the perfecting of the saints.* It is essential that the one love should bind and merge
all these into the unity of Christ's body, and
it is entirely incapable of doing this if it is not
itself regulated. For if each one is carried
away by his own impulse in accord with the
spirit he receives, and applies himself indif-
ferently to everything as he feels suggests
rather than as he judges by reason, until no
one is content with his assigned duty but all
simultaneously undertake to administer everything indiscriminately, there will clearly be no
unity but confusion instead.

III. 6. 'He set love in order in me.' Would
that the Lord Jesus would set in order in me
the little fund of love he gave me, that while
my interest may extend to all his concerns, I
may care before everything else for the pro-
ject or duty he has appointed especially for
me. My primary concern for this however
should be such that I may be drawn all the
more to the many things that do not especially pertain to me. For that which demands
first care does not always demand greater
love, since often the thing that we worry
about most is of no great use, and should not
constrain our love. So frequently what is
duty's first concern is less esteemed by the
judgement, and what truth considers of first
importance true love demands must be embraced more ardently. For example, does
duty not impose on me the care of all of you?

Now if by chance I should prefer to this work something that would prevent me striving with all my strength to execute it worthily and profitably, the principle of order would not approve it, even though I might seem to do it for love's sake. Yet if I apply myself as I ought to this charge before everything else, but fail to rejoice in the greater gains for God that I see another achieving, it is evident that I partially observe the order of love and partially do not. If however I reveal genuine concern for that which is my special charge, and nevertheless a still finer sympathy for a work that is greater, I find that I have fulfilled the order of love in both ways, and there is no reason why even I should not be able to say that 'he set love in order in me'.

7. Yet if you say it is hard for a person to rejoice more in another's great achievement than in his own small effort, you certainly perceive from this the excellence of the bride's grace, and that not every soul can say: 'he set love in order in me'. Why have the faces of some of you fallen at this statement? These deep sighs bear witness to a sad mind and dispirited conscience. Measuring ourselves against ourselves,* we feel, from the **2 Cor 10:12* experience of our own imperfection, some of us, how rare a virtue it is not to envy the virtue of another, not to mention rejoicing in it, not to mention that one should be all the more happy with himself the more he considers himself surpassed in virtue. There is yet a little light among us, brothers, as many of us feel this way about ourselves.

IV. Let us walk while we have the light,
lest darkness overtake us.* To walk is to make
progress. The apostle was walking when he
said: 'I do not consider that I have made it
my own;' and added: 'but one thing I do, forgetting what lies behind I strain forward to
what lies ahead.'* What is this one thing? One
thing, he says, has remained with me, as a
remedy, a hope, a consolation. What is it?
Evidently 'forgetting what lies behind I strain
forward to what lies ahead'. What sublime
confidence. That distinguished 'chosen instru-
ment',* denying that he is perfect, declares
that he is moving ahead! The danger therefore
is that not he who walks but he who takes his
ease will be overcome by the darkness of
death.* And who takes his ease but the man
who has no will to advance? Pay heed to this,
and if you die early, you will be at rest.*
You may say to God: 'Your eyes beheld my
imperfect being.' And nevertheless 'in your
book all shall be written.'* Who are all?
Surely those who possess the desire to advance. The text continues: 'days shall be
formed, and no one in them';* you supply:
shall perish. Understand 'days' as those who
are advancing, who, if they are surprised by
death, will be made perfect in that which is
lacking in them. They shall be formed, and
none among them left imperfect.

8. 'And how can I advance,' you say, 'I,
who am jealous of my brother's progress?' If
you grieve for your jealousy, you feel it without yielding to it. It is a passion that time will
heal, not an action to be condemned. But
you must not relax in it, plotting mischief in

Jn 12:35

Phil 3:13

Acts 9:15

Lk 1:79

Wis 4:7

Ps 138:16

Ibid.

your bed,* how to foster the disease, that is, how to pander to the contagion, how to persecute the innocent by disparaging his fine achievements, by discouraging, misrepresenting or obstructing his undertakings. Otherwise it does not injure the one who advances and strives for better things,* because it is no longer he who does it but the sin that dwells within him.* Condemnation therefore is not for him who does not give his body to wickedness,* nor his tongue to slander, nor any other part of his body to the infliction of damage or injury; on the contrary he is ashamed of his evil disposition, and strives to expel the deep-seated vice by continued confession, by tears, by prayer. And should he not succeed he is thereby more gentle toward others, more humble in himself. Can a wise man condemn the sensible person who has learned from the Lord to be gentle and humble of heart?* It must not be that we should find devoid of salvation one who follows the Saviour, the Church's bridegroom, our Lord, who is God blessed for ever.* Amen.

*Ps 35:5

*Phil 3:13

*Rom 7:20

*Rom 6:19

*Mt 11:29

*Rom 1:25

SERMON FIFTY

I. CONCERNING LOVE IN THE AFFECTIONS AND IN ACTION; THE LAW OF LOVE; AND WHY GOD COMMANDS IMPOSSIBLE THINGS. II. THE THREEFOLD LOVE OF THE FLESH, OF REASON AND OF WISDOM, AND THE TRANSPOSED ORDER OF LOVE IN ACTION. III. THE ORDER OF AFFECTIVE LOVE, THAT UNDERSTANDS ALL THINGS AS THEY ARE.

I. 1. **P**ERHAPS YOU EXPECT A DISCUSSION of the next verses, thinking that the verse just dealt with is finished. But I am working on something else, for I have still to set before you some left-overs from yesterday's feast that I collected to prevent them spoiling.* They will spoil if I give them to nobody: and if I wish to enjoy them alone, I myself shall be spoiled. I am unwilling then to keep them from that gullet of yours which I know so well, especially as they are presented from the tray of love, as sweet as they are delicate, as tasty as they are small. Furthermore it is altogether contrary to love to deprive people of love. So here I am: 'he has set love in order in me.'*

*Jn 6:12

*Sg 2:4

2. Love exists in action* and in feeling.† *actus
And with regard to love in action, I believe †affectus
that a law, an explicit commandment, has
been given to men;* yet how can one's feel- *Deut 5:6
ings correspond to the commandment? The
former therefore is commanded in view of
merit, the latter is given as a reward. We do
not deny that the present life, by divine
grace, can also experience its beginning and
progress, but we unreservedly maintain that
its consummation is in the happiness of the
life to come. How then should that be ordered which can in no way be fulfilled? Or if
you prefer to hold that affective love has
been commanded, I do not dispute it, provided you agree with me that in this life it
can never and will never be able to be fulfilled by any man. For who will dare to arrogate to himself what even Paul confessed he
did not comprehend?* The Lawgiver was not *Phil 3:13
unaware that the burden of the law exceeded
the powers of men, but he judged it useful for
this reason to advise men of their own insuffi-
ciency, that they might know the proper end
toward which they ought to strive according
to their powers. Therefore in commanding
impossible things he made men humble, not
prevaricators, so that every mouth may be
stopped and the whole world be made subject
to God, because nobody will be justified in
his sight by the works of the law.* Accepting *Rom 3:19-20
that command then, and conscious of our
deficiency, we shall cry to heaven and God
will have mercy on us.* And on that day we *1 Mac 4:10
shall know that God has saved us, not by the
righteous works that we ourselves have done,

*Tit 3:5

but according to his mercy.*

3. This is what I should say if we were agreed that affective [love] were a law commanded. But that seems especially to apply to [love in] action, because when the Lord said: 'Love your enemies', he referred right afterwards to actions: 'Do good to those who hate you.'* Scripture also says: 'If your enemy is hungry feed him; if he is thirsty, give him drink.'* Here you have a question of actions, not of feeling. But listen also to the Lord's command about love of himself: 'If you love me keep my words'.* And here too, by enjoining the observance of the commandments, he assigns us to action. It would have been superfluous for him to warn us to act if love were but a matter of feeling. Hence it is necessary that you accept as well that commandment to love your neighbor as yourself,* even if it is not expressed as clearly as this. Do you then consider that you do enough to fulfil the command to love of neighbor if you observe perfectly what the natural law prescribes for every man: 'What you would not wish done to yourself, avoid doing to another';* and also: 'Always treat others as you like them to treat you'?*

4. I am not saying that we should be without affection, and that with an arid heart we move only our hands to work. Among the many great and grievous evils that the apostle ascribes to men I have read this one is reckoned: to be without affection.*

II. But there is an affection which the flesh begets, and one which reason controls, and

*Lk 6:27

*Rom 12:20

*Jn 14:15

*Mt 22:39

*Tob 4:16,
RB 61
*Mt 7:12

*Rom 1:31,
2 Tim 3:3

one which wisdom seasons. The first is that which the apostle says is not subject to the law of God, nor can be;* the second, on the contrary, he shows to in agreement with the law of God because it is good*—one cannot doubt that the insubordinate and the agreeable differ from each other. The third, however, is far from either of them, because it tastes and experiences that the Lord is sweet;* it banishes the first and rewards the second. The first is pleasant, of course, but shameful; the second is emotionless but strong; the last is rich and delightful. Therefore by the second good deeds are done, and in it love reigns: not that of the feelings, which, growing richer with the seasoning of wisdom's salt,* fills the mind with a mighty abundance of the sweetness of the Lord,* but that rather which is practical, not yet indeed imparting the delightful refreshment of sweet love, but still vehemently aflame with the love of love itself. 'Do not love in word or speech,' he said, 'but in deed and in truth.'*

 5. Do you see how cautiously he takes a middle path between vitiated and affective love, while distinguishing from both the love that is active and salutary? He neither finds room in this love for the figment of a lying tongue, nor does he yet demand the flavor of loving wisdom. 'Let us love in deed and in truth',* he says, because we are moved to do good more by the vigorous urging of truth than by the feeling of relished love. 'He set love in order in me.'* Which of these loves do you think? Both of them, but in reverse order. Now the active prefers what is lowly, the

*Rom 8:7

*Rom 7:16

*Ps 33:9

*Col 4:6

*Ps 30:20

*1 Jn 3:18

*1 Jn 3:18

*Sg 2:4

affective what is lofty. For example, there is no doubt that in a mind that loves rightly, the love of God is valued more than love of men, and among men themselves the more perfect [is esteemed] more than the weaker, heaven more than earth, eternity more than the flesh. In well-regulated action, on the other hand, the opposite order frequently or even always prevails. For we are more strongly impelled toward and more often occupied with the welfare of our neighbor; we attend our weaker brothers with more exacting care; by human right and very necessity we concentrate more on peace on earth than on the glory of heaven;* by worrying about temporal cares we are not permitted to think of eternal things; in attending almost continually to the ills of our body we lay aside the care of our soul; and finally, in accord with the saying of the Apostle, we invest our weaker members with greater honor,* so fulfilling in a sense the word of the Lord: 'the last shall be first and the first last'.* Who will doubt that in prayer a man is speaking with God? But how often, at the call of charity, we are drawn away, torn away, for the sake of those who need to speak to us or be helped! How often does dutiful repose yield dutifully to the uproar of business! How often is a book laid aside in good conscience that we may sweat at manual work! How often for the sake of administering worldly affairs we very rightly omit even the solemn celebration of Masses! A preposterous order; but necessity knows no law. Love in action devises its own order, in

*Lk 2:14

*1 Cor 12:23

*Mt 20:16

accord with the command of the house-
holder, beginning with the most recent;* it is
certainly dutiful and correct, without favo-
ritism,* swayed not by worldly values but
by human needs.

*Mt 20:8

**Acts 10:34,
Job 32:21*

6. But not so affective love, since it always
leads the ordering from the first. It is the wisdom by which all things are experienced as they
are; as for example, the higher the nature the
more perfect the love it evokes; the lower
evokes less, the lowest nothing. The truth of
love determines the previous order, but this
order the love of truth lays claim to itself.
Now true love is found in this, that those
whose need is greater receive first;* and again
loving truth is evident if we maintain in our
feelings the order it maintains in the reason.

*1 Jn 4:10

III. But you, if you love the Lord your God
with your whole heart, whole mind, whole
strength,* and leaping with ardent feeling
beyond that love of love with which active
love is satisfied and having received the Spirit
in fullness, are wholly aflame with that
divine love to which the former is a step,
then God is indeed experienced, although
not as he truly is, a thing impossible for any
creature, but rather in relation to your power
to enjoy. Then you will experience as well
your own true self, since you perceive that
you possess nothing at all for which you love
yourself, except insofar as you belong to
God: you pour out upon him your whole
power of loving. I repeat: you experience
yourself as you are, when by that experience
of love of yourself and of the feeling that you

*Mk 12:30

feel toward him, you discover that you are an altogether unworthy object even of your own love, except for the sake of him without whom you are nothing.

7. As for your neighbor whom you are obliged to love as yourself:* if you are to experience him as he is, you will actually experience him only as you do yourself: he is what you are. You who do not love yourself then, except because you love God, consequently love as yourself all those who similarly love him. But you who love God cannot love as yourself a human enemy, for he is nothing in that as he does not love God;* yet you will love him so that he may love. But, to love in order that he may love, and to love because he loves, are not the same thing. That you may experience him as he is, therefore, you must experience him not for what he is, because he is nothing, but for what perhaps he will become, which is almost nothing since it still hangs in doubt. But when it becomes clear that he will not return to the love of God, it is essential that you regard him, not as almost nothing but as totally nothing, in that he will be eternally nothing. With this one exception, since not only is he not to be loved, but even to be looked on with hatred, in accord with the text: 'Lord, do I not hate those who hate you, and loathe those who defy you?'* the love that is open does not permit the refusal of some feeling, however small, to any man, even to one's greatest enemy. Who is wise enough to understand these things?*

8. Give me a man who loves God before

Mt 19:19

1 Jn 4:20

Ps 138:21

Ps 106:43

all things and with his whole being, self and neighbor in proportion to their love of God, the enemy as one who perhaps some day will love, his physical parents very deeply because of the natural bond, but his spiritual guides more generously because of grace. In like manner let him deal with the other things of God too with an ordered love, disregarding the earth, esteeming heaven, using this world as if not using it,* and discriminating between the things used and those enjoyed with an intimate savoring in his mind. Let him pay but passing attention to things that pass, as existing need demands. Let him embrace eternal things with an eternal desire. Give me such a man, I repeat, and I shall boldly proclaim him wise, because he appreciates things for what they really are, because he can truthfully and confidently boast and say: 'he set love in order in me.'* But where is he, and when shall these be? In tears I ask.* How long shall we smell and not taste, gazing toward the fatherland and not taking possession, sighing for it and saluting from afar? O Truth, fatherland of exiles, end of their exile! I see you, but held fast by the flesh I may not enter. Filthy with sins, I am not fit to be admitted. O Wisdom, reaching mightily from end to end in establishing and controlling things,* and arranging all things sweetly by enriching the affections and setting them in order! Guide our actions as your eternal truth requires, that each of us may confidently boast in you and say: 'he set love in order in me.'* For you are the strength of God and the Wisdom of God,* Christ

*1 Cor 7:31

*Sg 2:4
*Phil 3:18

*Wis 8:1

*Sg 2:4
*1 Cor 1:24

the Church's bridegroom, our Lord and God
Rom 1:25 who is blessed for ever. Amen.

SERMON FIFTY-ONE

I. CONCERNING THE FLOWERS AND
APPLES WITH WHICH THE CHURCH OR
FAITHFUL SOUL IS ENCOMPASSED.
II. HOW THE BRIDE ASKS TO BE SUS-
TAINED BY THE FAITH AND GOOD WORKS
OF THE MAIDENS WHILE THE BRIDE-
GROOM IS ABSENT. III. THE MEANING
OF THE BRIDEGROOM'S LEFT ARM AND
RIGHT ARM, AND WHAT FOLLOWS FROM
THIS STATEMENT. IV. WHEN THE
MIND HAS THE LEFT ARM UNDER THE
HEAD, WHEN ON THE HEAD, AND THE
ROLE OF HOPE.

I. 1. 'PROP ME UP WITH FLOWERS, encompass me with apples, because I
languish with love.'* Love has increased because the incentives to love have
occurred more often than usual. For you perceive on this occasion the abundant opportunities not only of seeing the bridegroom but
of conversing with him. The very sight of
him makes her happy with a serener coun-
tenance, his speech is more pleasant, his
conversation more prolonged and unhurried.
She is not only delighted with his conversation, but honored by his praise. Furthermore,
she is refreshed in his shadow she has so long

*Sg 2:5

39

desired, is nourished with his fruit, has drunk from his cup. We must not think that she came up thirsty from the wine-cellar, into which she so recently boasted she had been introduced;* and yet she is thirsty, because 'he who drinks me will thirst for more'.* After all these [experiences], when the bridegroom withdrew in his usual way, she says that she languishes with love,* meaning because of love. For the keener her joy in his presence, the more irksome her sense of his absence. The removal of what you love spells an increase of desire for it, and what you eagerly desire you miss painfully. Therefore in the meantime she asks to be comforted with the scents of flowers and fruits, until the return of him whose absence she so wearily endures. That is what the words' sequence conveys.

2. Now, under the Spirit's guidance, let us try to draw out the spiritual fruit contained in them. And if the speaker here is taken to be the Church, the communion of saints, it is we who are designated by the flowers and fruits, along with all those converted from a worldly life in the whole world. In the flowers we are shown the fresh and still tender life-style of beginners, and in the fruits the fortitude of those making progress, the maturity of the perfect. Surrounded by these, the pregnant and fruitful mother, for whom to live is Christ and to die is gain* bears with greater equanimity the irksomeness of her waiting, since, according to Scripture, she is given a share in what her hands have worked for,* in the first fruits of the Spirit,† and her works proclaim her praises in the city gates.

*Sg 2:4
*Sir 24:29

*Sg 2:5

*Phil 1:21

*Prov 31:31
†Rom 8:23

If, however, you want to attribute both of
these, the flowers and the fruit, to the one
person according to their moral sense, understand the flower as faith, the fruit as action.
Nor do I think that this will seem wrong to
you, if, just as the flower by necessity precedes the fruit, so faith ought to come before
good works.* Without faith, moreover, it is   *Heb 11:6
impossible to please God, as Paul attests. And
he even teaches that 'whatever does not
proceed from faith is sin'.* Hence there is   *Rom 14:23
neither fruit without a flower nor a good
work without faith. But then, faith without
good works is dead,* just as a flower seems   *Jas 2:20
vain where no fruit follows. 'Prop me up with
flowers, encompass me with apples, because I
languish with love.'* Therefore the mind   *Sg 2:5
accustomed to quietude receives consolation
from good works rooted in a sincere faith*   *1 Tim 1:5
whenever, as often happens, the light of contemplation is withdrawn. For who can enjoy
the light of contemplation—I do not say continually but even for long—while she remains
in the body? But, as I said, as often as she
falls away from contemplation she takes
refuge in action, from which she will surely
return to the former state as from an adjoin-
ing place, with greater intimacy, since these
two are comrades and live together: for
Martha is sister to Mary.* And though she   *Lk 10:39
loses the light of contemplation, she does not
permit herself to fall into the darkness of sin
or the idleness of sloth, but holds herself
within the light of good works. And that you
may know that good works are light Christ
said: 'Let your light shine before men';* and   *Mt 5:16

there is no doubt that this was said about works that men could see with their eyes.

II. 3. 'Prop me up with flowers, encompass me with apples, because I languish with love.' When that which is loved is at hand, love thrives; when absent it languishes. This is simply the weariness of impatient desire by which the mind of the ardent lover is necessarily afflicted when the loved one is absent; wholly absorbed in expectation, she reckons even any haste to be slow. And therefore she asks for an assortment of the fruits of good works made fragrant by faith in which she may rest while the bridegroom tarries.* I am telling you of what comes within my own experience. Whenever I discover that any of you have benefited from my admonitions, then I confess that I never regret preferring the preparation of my sermon to my personal leisure and quietude. When, for example, after a sermon the angry man is found to have become gentle, the proud man humble, the timid man brave; or when someone who is gentle, humble and brave has made progress in these gifts and admits that he is better than before; when those who perchance were lukewarm and tired of spiritual studies, benumbed and sleepy, are seen to grow eager and vigilant again through the burning words of the Lord; when those who, deserting the fountain of wisdom, have dug for themselves wells of self-will that cannot hold water* and, afflicted in consequence by every command, have been murmuring in dryness of heart because they possessed no moisture of devo-

*Mt 25:5

*Jer 2:13

tion*—when these, I repeat, are shown through the dew of the word and the abundant rain that God provides for those who are his,* to prosper again in works of obedience, to be prompt and devoted in all things, there is no reason for sorrow to invade the mind because it is interrupted in its pursuit of sweet contemplation, for I shall be surrounded by these flowers and fruits of love. Where the fruits of your progress grow in profusion about me I patiently accept being torn away from the unfruitful embraces of Rachel. The interruption of my leisure in order to prepare a sermon will not trouble me in the least when I shall see my seed germinating in you* and an increase in the growth of the harvest of your righteousness.* For love, which does not seek what is its own,* has long since easily convinced me not to prefer my own cherished desires to your gain. To pray, to read, to write, to meditate, or any other gains that may result from the study of spiritual things: these I consider loss because of you.*

4. 'Prop me up with flowers, encompass me with apples, because I languish with love.' This is what the bride said to the maidens in the bridegroom's absence, counselling them to advance in faith and good works till he comes,* knowing that this insured the approval of the bridegroom, the welfare of the maidens, and her own consolation. I know that I have explained this passage more fully in my book on the love of God,* and under another understanding. Whether it is better or worse, the reader may judge, if he cares to look up both. A prudent man will not con-

*Lk 8:6

*Ps 67:10

*Is 61:11

*2 Cor 9:10
*1 Cor 13:5

*Phil 3:7

*1 Cor 11:26

*On Loving God,
III, 7 (CF 13:
98-100)

demn me for this difference of meaning, just as long as the truth is upheld in both, and love, which the scriptures must serve, shall thereby build up more people as it draws from them more true understandings for its purpose.

III. 5. Then come the words: 'His left arm under my head, his right arm will embrace me'.* This too I remember having discussed elaborately in the work I mentioned:* but let me explain the sequence of this text. It is clear that the bridegroom has returned for the purpose of comforting the distressed bride by his presence. How could she who had been prostrated by his absence not grow strong in his presence? Therefore he does not tolerate the affliction of his beloved. He is at her side, nor can he delay when summoned by desires so great. And because he found that during his absence she had been faithful in good works and eager for gain, in that she had ordered that flowers and fruits to given to her, of course, he returns this time with an even richer reward of grace. As she lies back he cushions her head on one of his arms, embracing her with the other, to cherish her at his bosom. Happy the soul who reclines on the breast of Christ,* and rests between the arms of the Word! 'His left arm under my head, his right arm will embrace me.' She does not say 'embraces', but 'will embrace me', to show that far from being ungrateful for the first grace, she anticipates the second by giving thanks.

6. Learn not to be tardy or sluggish in

*Sg 2:6

*On Loving God, III, 10 and IV, 12-13 (CF 13: 102, 105-106)

*Jn 13:25

offering thanks, learn to offer thanks for each
and every gift. Take careful note, scripture
advises, of what is set before you,* so that   *Prov 23:1
no gift of God, be it great or mediocre or
small, will be deprived of due thanksgiving.
We are even commanded to gather up the
fragments, lest they be lost,* which means   *Jn 6:12
that we are not to forget even the smallest
benefits. Is that surely not lost which is given
to an ingrate? Ingratitude is the soul's enemy,
a voiding of merits, dissipation of the virtues,
wastage of benefits. Ingratitude is a burning
wind that dries up the source of love, the dew
of mercy, the streams of grace. For this reason the bride, as soon as she sensed the grace
of his left hand, offered thanks without waiting for the teeming fulness in his right. For
on mentioning that his left hand was under
her head, she did not go on to say that she
was embraced at the same time by his right.
She said rather it 'will embrace me'.

7. What more are we to think the left
hand and the right are for the bridegroom,
the Word? Does that which is called the word
of man have within it separate bodily parts,
distinct features, and a difference between
the left side and the right? All the more does
he who is God and the Word of God not ad-
mit diversity of any kind, he is who he is,* so   *Ex 3:14
simple in his nature that he has no parts, so
much one that he is without number. For he
is the wisdom of God,* of whom it is   *1 Cor 1:24
written: his wisdom is beyond numbering.*   *Ps 146:5
But that which is unchangeable is incompre-
hensible, and hence cannot be expressed in
language. Where, I ask, can you find the

words to pay worthy tribute to that majesty, or properly describe it, or adequately define it? But we speak as well as we can of that which we do our best to understand, as the Holy Spirit reveals. We are taught by the authority of the Fathers and the usage of the scriptures that it is lawful to appropriate suitable analogies from the things we know, and rather than coin new words, to borrow the familiar with which these analogies may be worthily and properly clothed. Otherwise you will make an absurd attempt to teach the unknown by the unknown.

8. Therefore, as adversity and prosperity are usually designated by the left hand and by the right, it seems to me that here the left may be interpreted as the Word's threat of punishment, the right as his promise of the kingdom.

IV. Now there are times when our mind is slavishly oppressed by the fear of punishment; and then the left arm can be said to be by no means under the head but on the head; anyone so afflicted cannot say at all that 'his left arm is under my head'.* But if, abandoning this slavish attitude,* he passes over to a worthier disposition of spontaneous service, insofar as he is rather challenged by the rewards than coerced by penalties, especially if he is inspired by love of the good itself, then certainly he can say: 'his left arm is under my head'. Anyone who has overcome that slavish fear which is in the left arm by a better, more excellent habit of mind, and by worthy desires has drawn near to the right

*Sg 2:6
*Rom 8:15

arm which holds the promises, can say to the Lord with the prophet: 'in your right hand are everlasting pleasures'.* This engenders the hope by which she confidently asserts: 'his right arm will embrace me.'* *Ps 15:11*

Sg 2:6

9. Consider with me now whether one so disposed, one who has attained a position of such great happiness, may not suitably apply to herself the words of the psalm and say: 'I will lie down in peace and take my rest',* *Ps 4:9* especially when the reason which follows is present: 'For you alone, O Lord, make me rest secure'.* That's how it is. As long as one *Ps 4:10* is oppressed by a slavish spirit, one has little hope and much fear. He enjoys neither peace nor rest as his conscience wavers between hope and because he is greatly tormented by the fear of supreme excellence, 'fear expects punishment'.* And so it is not for him to *1 Jn 4:18* say: 'I will lie down in peace and take my rest',* for he cannot as yet say that he is *Ps 4:9* firmly established in hope. But if, with an increase of grace, fear begins to diminish and hope to grow strong, until finally he comes to a state where perfect love entirely casts out fear,* will a soul of this kind not seem *1 Jn 4:18* firmly established in hope, and thereby to lie down in peace and rest?

10. 'If you sleep in the middle of the chosen lots, there are dove-wings covered with silver.'* What I think this means is that *Ps 67:14* there is a place between fear and security like that between the left arm and the right, a central hope, as it were, in which the mind and conscience very happily repose on the soft bed of love. And perhaps this place is

referred to in a subsequent text of this Song, where in a description of the throne of Solomon you have the following: 'the midst he covered with love for the daughters of Jerusalem.'* Now anyone who feels that he is firmly established in hope no longer serves in fear but rests in love. So the bride rests and sleeps, and for her sake he says: 'I adjure you, O daughters of Jerusalem, by the gazelles and hinds of the fields, that you stir not up nor awaken the beloved until she pleases'.* Great and awesome concern, that he lets the soul which contemplates repose on his breast, He even guards her from intrusive cares, and protects her from disquieting action and the pressures of business. He does not permit her to be awakened except at her own wish. But this should not be examined within the confines of a sermon's conclusion. Better that it be resumed at another time, lest a theme so attractive be deprived of the diligence it deserves in its treatment. 'Not that we are sufficient of ourselves to claim anything as coming from us' even then, especially in a matter so worthy, so excellent, so entirely supereminent; 'But our sufficiency is from God',* the bridegroom of the Church, our Lord Jesus Christ, who is God blessed for ever.* Amen.

*Sg 3:9-10

*Sg 2:7

*2 Cor 3:5

*Rom 1:25

SERMON FIFTY-TWO

I. GOD'S ESTEEM FOR THE ONE HE
LOVES IS EXPRESSED IN THE OPENING
WORDS OF THIS SERMON. II. THE
SLEEP OF THE BRIDE, FROM WHICH THE
BRIDEGROOM FORBIDS THAT SHE BE
WAKENED. III. ECSTASY OF THIS KIND
MAY IN A SPECIAL WAY BE CALLED
CONTEMPLATION. IV. WHO ARE THE
GAZELLES AND HINDS OF THE FIELDS?
THE MAIDENS ARE WARNED NOT TO
DISTURB THE BELOVED NEEDLESSLY.

I. 1. 'I CHARGE YOU, daughters of Jerusalem, by the gazelles and hinds of
the fields, not to stir my beloved or
rouse her until she pleases.'* This is a prohibi-   *Sg 2:7
tion to the maidens whom he calls 'daughters
of Jerusalem', because, although they are
delicate and tender, their feminine appetites
and conduct still untempered, they nevertheless cling to the bride in the hope of making
progress and reaching Jerusalem. They are
forbidden therefore to disturb the sleeping
bride or to presume to awaken her against
her will. Hence her completely tender bridegroom supports her head with his left arm,*   *Sg 2:6
as has been already said, to enable her to relax
and sleep on his breast. And now, as Scripture

49

goes on to say, he keeps guard over her with all courtesy and affection, lest she be molested and wakened by the frequent and petty demands of the maidens. This is the literal sense of the text. But that attestation, 'by the gazelles and hinds of the fields', taken literally, seems entirely devoid of rational meaning, so totally does it demand a spiritual interpretation. But however this may be, in the meantime 'it is good for us to be here'* and to gaze briefly on the goodness of the divine nature, its sweetness and courtesy. For what human affections have you ever experienced, any of you, that are sweeter than is now expressed to you from the heart of the Most High? And it is expressed by him who searches the depths of God,* who cannot but know what is in him, because he is his Spirit. Nor can he say openly anything except what he sees in him, for he is the Spirit of Truth.*

2. Actually our race is not without someone who happily deserved to enjoy this gift, who experienced within herself this sweetest mystery, unless we entirely disbelieve the passage of scripture we have at hand, where the heavenly bridegroom is plainly shown as passionately defending the repose of his beloved, eager to embrace her within his arms as she sleeps, lest she be roused from her delicious slumber by annoyance or disquiet I cannot restrain my joy that this majesty did not disdain to bend down to our weakness in a companionship so familiar and sweet, that the supreme Godhead did not scorn to enter into wedlock with the soul in exile and to reveal to her with the most

*Mt 17:4

*1 Cor 2:10

*Jn 16:13

ardent love how affectionate was this bridegroom whom she had won. That in heaven it is
like this, as I read on earth, I do not doubt,
nor that the soul will experience for certain
what this page suggests, except that here she
cannot fully express what she will there be
capable of grasping, but cannot yet grasp.
What do you think she will receive there,
when now she is favored with an intimacy so
great as to feel herself embraced by the
arms of God, cherished on the breast of God,
guarded by the care and zeal of God lest she
be roused from her sleep by anyone till she
wakes of her own accord.

II. 3. Well then, let me explain if I can what
this sleep is which the bridegroom wishes his
beloved to enjoy, from which he will not
allow her to be wakened under any circum-
stances, except at her good pleasure; for if
someone should read the apostle's words: 'it
is full time now for you to wake from
sleep',* or read how God was asked by the   *Rom 13:11
prophet to enlighten his eyes lest he sleep the
sleep of death,* he might be troubled by the   *Ps 12:4
ambiguity of the words and be entirely unable to form any worthy sentiments about the
sleep of the bride that is here described. Nor
does it resemble that sleep of Lazarus which
the Lord mentions in the Gospel: 'Our
friend Lazarus has fallen asleep, but I go to
wake him out of sleep'.* He said this about   *Jn 11:11
the death of his body,* though the disciples   *Jn 2:21
were thinking of sleep. This sleep of the
bride, however, is not the tranquil repose of
the body that for a time sweetly lulls the

fleshly senses, nor that dreaded sleep whose custom is to take life away completely. Farther still is it removed from that deathly sleep by which a man perseveres irrevocably in sin and so dies.* It is a slumber which is vital and watchful, which enlightens the heart, drives away death, and communicates eternal life. For it is a genuine sleep that yet does not stupefy the mind but transports it. And— I say it without hesitation—it is a death, for the apostle Paul in praising people still living in the flesh spoke thus: 'For you have died, and your life is hid with Christ in God.'*

4. It is not absurd for me to call the bride's ecstasy a death, then, but one that snatches away not life but life's snares, so that one can say: 'We have escaped as a bird from the snare of the fowlers'.* In this life we move about surrounded by traps, but these cause no fear when the soul is drawn out of itself by a thought that is both powerful and holy, provided that it so separates itself and flies away from the mind that it transcends the normal manner and habit of thinking; for a net is spread in vain before the eyes of winged creatures.* Why dread wantonness where there is no awareness of life? For since the ecstatic soul is cut off from awareness of life though not from life itself, it must of necessity be cut off from the temptations of life. 'O that I had wings like a dove! I would fly away and be at rest.'* How I long often to be the victim of this death that I may escape the snares of death,* that I may not feel the deadening blandishments of a sensual life, that I may be steeled against evil

*1 Jn 2:21

*Col 3:3

*Ps 123:7

*Prov 1:17

*Ps 54:7

*Ps 17:6

desire, against the surge of cupidity, against the goads of anger and impatience, against the anguish of worry and the miseries of care. Let me die the death of the just,* that no injustice may ensnare or wickedness seduce me. How good the death that does not take away life but makes it better; good in that the body does not perish but the soul is exalted. *Num 23:10

5. Men alone experience this. But, if I may say so, let me die the death of angels that, transcending the memory of things present, I may cast off not only the desire for what are corporeal and inferior but even their images, that I may enjoy pure conversation with those who bear the likeness of purity.

III. This kind of ecstasy, in my opinion, is alone or principally called contemplation. Not to be gripped during life by material desires is a mark of human virtue; but to gaze without the use of bodily likenesses is the sign of angelic purity. Each, however, is a divine gift, each is a going out of oneself, each a transcending of self, but in one one goes much farther than in the other. Happy the man who can say: 'See, I have escaped far away, and found a refuge in the wilderness'.* *Ps 54:8 He was not satisfied with going out if he could not go far away, so that he could be at rest. You have so over-leaped the pleasures of the flesh that you are no longer responsive to its concupiscence* even in the least, nor gripped *Rom 6:12 by its allure. You have advanced, you have placed yourself apart, but you have not yet

*Is 66:1

put yourself at a distance, unless you succeed in flying with purity of mind beyond the material images that press in from every side. Until that point promise yourself no rest. You err if you expect to find before then a place of rest,* the privacy of solitude, unclouded light, the abode of peace. But show me the man who has attained to this and I shall promptly declare him to be at rest. Rightly may he say: 'Return, O my soul, to your rest; for the Lord has dealt bountifully with you.'* For this place is truly a solitude where one dwells in the light, precisely what the prophet calls 'a shade by day from the heat, a refuge and a shelter from rain and tempest';* or as holy David said: 'He hid me in his shelter in the day of trouble, he concealed me under the cover of his tent.'*

*Ps 114:7

*Is 4:6

*Ps 26:5

6. Consider therefore that the bride has retired to this solitude, there, overcome by the loveliness of the place, she sweetly sleeps within the arms of her bridegroom, in ecstasy of spirit. Hence the maidens are forbidden to waken her until she herself pleases. But how forbidden?

IV. This is no straightforward prohibition nor the customary mild warning, but an entirely new and unusual adjuration, namely, 'by the gazelles and hinds of the fields'.* It seems to me that these animals, because of their sharpness of vision and swiftness of motion, fittingly designate both the holy souls who have laid aside the body and the angels who are in God's presence. We know that these qualities belong to those spirits;

*Sg 2:7

they easily soar to the heights and penetrate
secret things. Again, the life [the animals]
live in the fields obviously points to the free
and graceful discourse of [the angels'] contemplation. What is their part then in this
solemn appeal? Surely that the restless maidens may not dare, through fickleness, to recall
his beloved from the sublime company to
which she is introduced as often as she becomes ecstatic in contemplation. And so
they are justly intimidated by the authority
of those from whose company their impor-
tunity would snatch her away. Let the maidens realize whom they offend when they
disturb their mother, and beware of so pre-
suming on her maternal love that without real
necessity they intrude on that heavenly encounter. Let them realize that this is what
they do when without justification they
trouble a person resting in contemplation.
Since she is not allowed to be aroused
by them until she pleases, it is for her to
choose both when to be at leisure and when
to devote attention to them. The bridegroom
knows how ardently the bride glows with
love for her neighbors too, how her own love
amply prompts her maternal interest in her
daughters' progress, and that she will neither
withdraw from nor refuse to go to them when
they need her. Hence he judged that manage-
ment of those affairs might be safely com-
mitted to her discretion. For she is not one of
the many marked down by the prophet's
withering scorn, those who take possession of
the fat and the strong and reject the weak.*   *Ezek 34:3*
Does a doctor visit the healthy, and not more

*Mt 9:12

the sick?* And if he does, it is more as a friend than as a doctor. Good master, whom will you teach if you drive away all the

*Mt 19:16

untaught?* In whom, I ask, will you inculcate discipline, if you banish all the wayward, or fly from them? Among whom will you test your patience if you receive the gentle only, and exclude the willful?

*Mt 16:28

7. There are some sitting here* whom I wish to see paying greater attention to this present chapter. They should certainly ponder the deference owed to superiors, for by rashly disturbing them they become offensive even to those who dwell in heaven; and then at length they might begin to spare me a little bit more than hitherto, and not intrude so rudely and irresponsibly on my leisure. As they well know, rare is the hour in which I can relax from visitors, even when they themselves support me very patiently. I make this complaint reluctantly, however, for some timid person may conceal his needs and overtax his powers of endurance through fear of disturbing me. And so I desist, lest I seem to give an example of impatience to the weak.

*Mt 18:6

They are little ones of the Lord,* putting their trust in him; I shall not permit them to be

*1 Cor 9:12

scandalized by me.* I shall not use my authority; rather let them use me as they

*1 Cor 10:33

please, provided they attain salvation.* They will spare me by not sparing me, and I shall rest more in knowing that they are not afraid to trouble me about their needs. I shall

*Ps 145:2

accommodate myself to them as far as I can,* and as long as I live I shall serve God in them,

*2 Cor 6:6

in unfeigned love.* Let me not seek my own

advantage;* it is what is useful not to me but
to many that I shall judge useful for myself.*
This only I pray for, that my ministry may be
pleasing to them and fruitful, and perhaps in
time of evil I may, because of this, find
mercy in their Father's eyes, and in those of
the Church's bridegroom, our Lord Jesus
Christ, who with him is above all things, God
blessed for ever.*

*1 Cor 13:5
*1 Cor 10:33

*Rom 1:25

SERMON FIFTY-THREE

I. THE SEQUENCE OF THE TEXT: 'THE VOICE OF THE BELOVED'; HEARING PRE- CEDES SEEING. II. WHO THE MOUN- TAINS AND HILLS ARE OVER WHICH THE BRIDEGROOM LEAPS AND BOUNDS. III. HOW THE MOUNTAINS AND THE SHEEP, THAT IS THE HEAVENLY CITI- ZENS, ARE THE SAME. IV. THE MEAN- ING OF THE BRIDEGROOM'S LEAPINGS BY WHICH HE BOUNDS OVER THE MOUNTAINS.

*Sg 2:8

'THE VOICE OF MY BELOVED.'*
I. 1. When the bride becomes aware of the unusual shyness of the maidens, a timidity so respectful that they do not dare to intrude on her holy leisure, nor, unlike yesterday and the day before, presume to molest her in her contemplative repose, she recognizes it as the fruit of the bridegroom's care and service. And full of spiritual joy,* either because of their progress in curbing their excessive and superfluous levity, or be- cause her future repose will be thenceforward unimpeded, or even because of the bride- groom's esteem and favor revealed in his zeal for this repose of hers, in his eager defence of a leisure so delightful and so filled with

*Lk 10:21

fervor, she declares that it has been accomplished by the voice of her beloved directed to them for this purpose. For the man who presides with responsibility over others* **Rom 12:8* rarely if ever rests securely alone with himself, while he perpetually fears that he is removing himself from his brothers and failing to please God by preferring the pleasure of his own contemplative repose to the common good. At times, however, joy and comfort in good measure are the lot of him who rests in these delights, when, from a certain awe and respect for him divinely instilled in the hearts of his brothers, he understands that his repose is pleasing to God who enables them to support their needs with composure rather than rashly presume to disturb the rest so appreciated by their spiritual father. Now the proper fear of children is a manifest sign that they have inwardly heard that voice full of menace and rebuke that speaks through the prophet: 'It is I who announce righteousness.'* It is his voice, his **Is 63:1* inspiration, the onslaught of a righteous fear.

2. Having identified the voice therefore, the bride exults with joy saying: 'the voice of my beloved.' She is a friend and 'rejoices with great joy at the bridegroom's voice'.* **Jn 3:29* And she continues: 'See how he comes leaping upon the mountains, bounding over the hills.'* Being certain of the beloved's pre- **Sg 2:8* sence from the sound of his voice, she at once, unerringly, turns inquisitive eyes to see him whom she has heard. Hearing leads to sight; 'faith comes from what is heard'.* By **Rom 10:17* it hearts are so cleansed that God can be

*Acts 15:9

seen; hence you have the expression: 'cleansing hearts by faith'.* Accordingly she sees him coming after hearing his voice. Even the Holy Spirit maintains here the order which the prophet thus described: 'Hear O daughter, and see'.* And to convince you more surely that it is neither by accident nor by chance but by deliberate purpose and for the reason we have already alleged that hearing in this context is put before sight, take note whether this order of words was not also observed by the holy man who spoke as follows to God: 'I had heard of you by the hearing of the ear, but now my eye sees you.'* But again when we recall the Holy Spirit's descent on the apostles on the day of Pentecost, is not hearing presented as a prelude to sight? The text says: 'Suddenly a sound came from Heaven like the rush of a mighty wind';* after which 'There appeared to them tongues as of fire.'* Here the coming of the Holy Spirit is said to have been perceived first by hearing, then by sight. But enough on this, since you too, if you try to concentrate on this line of research, can perhaps find similar passages in other parts of scripture.

*Ps 44:11

*Job 42:5

*Acts 2:2

*Acts 2:3

II. 3. Now let us consider that point which demands more diligent research and whose meaning is more difficult of access. For this I confess my absolute need of the help of the Holy Spirit, that I may throw light on the significance of those mountains and hills over which the Church beheld with joy her bridegroom leaping and bounding, hastening to the redemption of her whose beauty he had

desired.* I am convinced beyond doubt that   *Ps 44:12
this is so, because I recall a similar passage
from the prophet who clearly foresaw in
spirit and foretold the coming of the Saviour:
'He pitched his tent in the sun, and comes
out of his pavilion like a bridegroom. He
exulted like a giant to run his race: his going
out is from the highest heavens and his cir-
cuit touches their farthest ends.'* The journey   *Ps 18:6-7
and the return are well known; by whom
begun and brought to completion, and why,
are also very well known. What then? Whether our reading be in the psalms or in the
present song, shall we imagine for ourselves a
powerful man of great stature, captivated by
the love of an absent girl-friend and hastening
to her desired embraces by bounding over
those mountains and hills whose massive bulk
we see towering to such heights above the
plain that the peaks of some seem to penetrate the clouds? Surely it will not do to fabricate physical images of this kind, especially
when treating of this spiritual Song; and it is
certainly not legitimate for us who recall
reading in the Gospel that 'God is a spirit and
those who worship him must worship in
spirit'.*   *Jn 4:24

4. Who then are those spiritual mountains
and hills? When we know this we may in consequence understand how the bridegroom
—who is God and therefore a spirit—leapt
upon and over them, and what the leapings
mean. If we consider them as those in which,
according to the Gospel, the ninety-nine
sheep were left behind while their dutiful
shepherd came on earth to seek the one which

*Mt 18:11-12

was lost,* the matter remains no less obscure and the mind is baffled, for it is difficult to ascertain who and of what nature are those spiritual mountains and hills in which the spiritual and happy citizens of high heaven dwell and feel—for undoubtedly they are the sheep who stay there. If they had no real existence Truth would not have said this. Nor long before that would the prophet have alleged of the Jerusalem that is above that 'its foundations are in the holy mountains',* if no holy mountains were there. And finally, that this heavenly dwelling-place really possesses not only spiritual but also living and intellectual mountains and hills, listen to Isaiah: 'The mountains and hills will sing praises before God.'*

*Ps 86:1

*Is 55:12

5. Who are they then, but those same spiritual inhabitants of heaven who, as we said, were named sheep by the Lord's voice, so that the sheep are mountains, though it may seem absurd to say that the mountains feed on mountains or the sheep on sheep?

III. Taken literally it does indeed seem uncouth; but in its spiritual sense it has a delightful flavor if we examine with sensitivity how the shepherd of both flocks,* namely Christ the Wisdom of God,* serves the same food of truth in one way to the sheep on earth, in another way to those in heaven. For we mortal men, while living as pilgrims,* are compelled to eat our bread in the sweat of our brow,* begging it from without with hardship and anguish,* that is, either from learned men or holy books, or certainly in those things

*Jn 10:2
*1 Cor 1:24

*Ps 118:54

*Gen 3:19
*2 Cor 11:27

that are made, seeing the invisible, under-
standable attributes of God.* Angels however receive it in all fullness, though not from
themselves, with a facility as great as the
happiness by which they live. For they are all
taught of God.* It is promised as certain
truth that those chosen from among men will
one day attain to this; as yet they cannot
enjoy it with secure happiness.

6. The mountains therefore feed on mountains and the sheep on sheep when the
spiritual creatures of heaven—themselves both
the mountains and the sheep—find abundantly
within themselves, from the Word of life,* the
means of perpetuating their blessed life. They
are mountains because of their loftiness and
fullness, sheep because of their gentleness.
Filled with God, made sublime with rewards,
adorned with virtues though they be, they
nevertheless yield and bow their lofty heads
in total and humble obedience to the rule of
him who utterly transcends them in majesty.
Like the gentlest of sheep they do at all
times what their shepherd wills, following
him wherever he goes.* These, in the prophet
David's words, are the real holy mountains,*
and on them, as on wisdom the first of all
things made,* the foundations of the city of
God stand firmly fixed from the beginning.
Though in part reigning in heaven and in part
pilgrimaging on earth, it is still one city. And
nevertheless, according to Isaiah, from these
as from sweetly echoing cymbals* the song
of praise and thanksgiving is ever resounding,*
fulfilling in this lovely and unceasing song
words we previously recalled from the same

*Rom 1:20

*Jn 6:45, Is 54:13

*1 Jn 1:1

*Rev 14:4
*Ps 86:1

*Sir 1:4

*Ps 150:5
*Is 51:3

prophet: 'The mountains and hills will sing praises before God';* and also those words which the psalmist spoke to the Lord God: 'Happy are those who dwell in your house O Lord! They will praise you for ever and ever.'*

*Is 55:12

*Ps 83:5

7. To return to that from which we digressed a little—though necessarily I think—these then are the mountains and hills over which the Church saw her heavenly bridegroom leaping with astounding swiftness as he sped to her embraces: and not only leaping but bounding over them.

IV. Do you want me to show you these leapings from the words of the prophets and apostles? Not that I intend now to disclose everything on this matter, since those who have time may go to the sources for it. It takes a long time, and is not necessary. I propose only what seems to support briefly and clearly the references to the leapings of the bridegroom. David says of him that 'he pitched his tent in the sun, and comes out of his pavilion like a bridegroom. He exulted like a giant to run his race: his going out is from the highest heavens.'* What a leap he made from the highest heavens to the earth! Indeed I can discover no place, other than the earth, where he would pitch his tent in the sun: that is, where he who dwells in unapproachable light* would deign to reveal his presence openly and in the light. For 'he appeared upon earth and lived among men'.* Upon earth, I say, in plain sight, which is meant by pitching his tent in the sun, namely, in the body which he was pleased to prepare for himself

*Ps 18:6-7

*1 Tim 6:16

*Bar 3:38

for this purpose from the Virgin's body,* that in it he who is by nature invisible might be seen, and so all mankind should see the salvation of God* on his coming in the flesh.*

*Heb 10:5

*Lk 3:6
*Jn 2:4

8. He leapt therefore upon the mountains, upon the highest angels, when he descended to them, graciously revealing to them the mystery hidden throughout the ages;* the great mystery of devotion.† But passing over these higher and more renowned mountains, the Cherubim and Seraphim, the Dominations, Principalities, Powers and Virtues,* he was pleased to come down, all the way down to the hills, even to the lowest angels. But did he remain upon them? He bounded over even the hills. For it was not the angels but the seed of Abraham that he took to himself,* a state even lower than the angels, that the word might be fulfilled which the prophet just mentioned said to the Father about the Son: 'You have made him a little less than the angels.'* Although this could be understood as praise of human nature, since man is made in the image and likeness of God* and endowed with reason even as an angel, he is yet a little less than the angel because of his earthly body. But listen to what the apostle Paul pointedly says of Christ: 'Though he was in the form of God, he did not count equality with God a thing to be grasped, but emptied himself, taking the form of a servant, being born in the likeness of men and in condition found as a man';* and again: 'when the time had fully come, God sent his Son, born of woman, born under the law, to

*Eph 3:9
†1 Tim 3:16

*Col 1:16

*Heb 2:16

*Ps 8:6

*Gen 1:26

*Phil 2:6

*Gal 4:4-5

redeem those who were under the law.'* He
then who was born of woman, born under the
law, in his downward flight not only bounded
over the mountains, that is over the greater
and higher spirits, but also over the lower
angels, who when compared with those above
them are rightly named hills. But he who is

*Lk 7:28

least in the kingdom of heaven* is greater
than anyone living bodily on earth, even if
he should be the great John the Baptist. For
although we confess that God made man is
far above and incomparably superior to every

*Eph 1:21

Principality and Power even in his manhood,*
yet it is certain that even if he surpasses them
in majesty he falls short of them in his weakness. And so he leapt upon the mountains,
bounded over the hills when he graciously
manifested himself as inferior not only to the
higher angels but even to the lower ones. Nor
was it to the spirits of heaven only that he
subjected himself, but also to those who dwell

*Job 4:19

in houses of clay,* bounding over and exceed-
ing by his lowliness even the lowliness of men.
As a boy in Nazareth he was obedient to

*Lk 2:51

Mary and Joseph,* and at the Jordan, in his
youthful manhood, he bowed beneath the

*Mt 3:13
*Lk 24:29

hands of John.* But the day is moving
on,* and we may not yet descend from these
mountains.

9. And so, if for the occasion we should
wish to investigate at our pleasure all these
things of beauty, to search into secret things,
we must fear that the sermon will either lack
becoming brevity or that a matter so excellent and promising will be deprived by hasti-
ness of due consideration. If you agree, then

let us rest here today in these mountains,
because it is good for us to be here,*   *Mt 17:4*
gathered by Christ together with the holy
angels in a place of pasture,* to be fed with   *Ps 22:2*
sweeter and richer fare. For we are indeed the
flock of his pasture.* Like 'clean animals'   *Ps 78:13*
therefore,* let us ruminate the repast from the   *Deut 14:7*
Good Shepherd, what we have swallowed
down so greedily in today's sermon, all the
more eager to lay hold in another sermon on
what remains of this text, by the generosity
of the Church's bridegroom, Jesus Christ Our
Lord, who is over all things God, blessed for
ever.* Amen.   *Rom 9:5*

SERMON FIFTY-FOUR

I. ANOTHER INTERPRETATION OF THE AFORESAID MOUNTAINS; THE BRIDE-GROOM LEAPS AMONG THEM WHEN HE USES THEM AS MINISTERS. II. THE HILLS OVER WHICH THE BRIDEGROOM LEAPS ARE SPIRITS OF THE AIR, DESIG-NATED BY GILBOA. III. FOR HIS PUNISHMENT THE DEVIL HAS BEEN ASSIGNED A PLACE IN THE AIR, BETWEEN THE HIGHER AND LOWER MOUNTAINS. IV. AN EXHORTATION TO BEWARE OF PRIDE, ACCORDING TO THE EXAMPLE OF THE ANGEL INDICATED BY GILBOA. V. THE THREEFOLD FEAR THAT MUST BE OURS, IF WE ARE TO AVOID PRIDE.

I. 1.   TODAY I AM GOING TO PRO-POSE another interpretation of the same verse that was dealt with in yesterday's sermon. Think them over and choose the better. There is no need to repeat yesterday's points, they could not have been forgotten so soon. But in case they have been, they were written down as they were de-livered, taken down by pen like the other sermons, so that what may slip the memory may easily be recovered. So here is the new matter. 'See how he comes', she says, 'leaping

68

upon the mountains, bounding over the hills.'* *Sg 2:8
She speaks of the bridegroom, who was certainly leaping upon the mountains when, sent
by the Father to preach the good news to the
poor,* he did not disdain to perform the task *Lk 4:18
of the angels: he who was the Lord became
the angel of great counsel.* He whose custom *Is 9:6
was to delegate others, himself descended to
the earth. The Lord himself made known his
salvation; he himself revealed his righteousness in the sight of the nations.* Since there- *Ps 97:2
fore, according to Paul's statement, 'they are
all ministering spirits, sent to help those who
will be the heirs of salvation',* he who was *Heb 1:14
superior to them became as one of them
among them,* disregarding their offence and *Gen 3:22
bestowing abundant grace. But listen to him.
'I came', he said, 'not to be served but to
serve, and to give my life as a ransom for
many.'* This is what none of the others is *Mt 20:28
found to have done: by his services both
dedicated and faithful, he has surpassed all
others who were seen to serve. He is the good
servant who served his flesh as food, his blood
as drink,* his life as ransom. Plainly good, *Jn 6:56
energetic in spirit, fervent in love, devoted in
affection, he not only leapt upon the mountains, but bounded over the hills, that is, he
triumphed and vanquished by his swiftness of
service, for he it was whom God, his God,
anointed with the oil of gladness above his
fellows;* in him he uniquely rejoiced like a *Ps 44:8
giant to run his course.* For he bounded over *Ps 18:6
Gabriel and preceded him to the Virgin, as the
archangel himself witnesses when he says:
'Hail, Mary, full of grace; the Lord is with

*Lk 1:28

you.'* What is this? He whom you just left in
heaven do you now find in the womb? He
flew, even flew ahead, on the wings of the
Ps 17:11 wind. You are beaten, O Archangel, over-
leapt by him who sent you ahead.

2. When he appeared in the angels long
ago to the patriarchs, he was surely leaping in
the mountains, which seems more in accord
with the letter of the text. It does not say
in montes 'leaping upon the mountains', but 'in the
in montibus mountains', so that he who causes and
enables them to leap would appear himself to
leap in them, just as he speaks in the prophets
and works in the righteous when he supplies
words to the former and deeds to the latter.
Furthermore, some of them represented him
in person, so that each of these spoke not as
an angel but as the Lord. For example, the
angel who spoke to Moses did not say 'I
Ex 10:2, 31:13 the Lord's', but 'I, the Lord', and repeated
this frequently. Therefore he was leaping in
the mountains, that is, in the angels, in whom
he both spoke and revealed his presence to
men. For he leaped down to men, but *in* the
angels, not in himself; not in his own nature
but in a subject creature. For anyone who
leaps goes from place to place, which does not
happen to God. And so he who could not
leap in himself leapt in the mountains, that is,
in the angels; and he leapt even to the hills, to
the patriarchs and prophets and other spiritual men on earth. But he bounded over the
hills too when he chose to speak and manifest
himself in the angels not only to great and
spiritual men, but to ordinary people, and
even to women.

II. Or perhaps hills mean the powers of the air that are no longer classed as mountains, since through pride they fell from the loftiness of the virtues, but have not yet subsided through penitence to the lowly ways of the valleys, or to the valleys of the lowly. It was about these that I think the psalmist said: 'The mountains melt like wax before the Lord.'* He who leapt upon the mountains surely bounded over these bloated and barren hills, situated between the mountains of the perfect and the valleys of the penitent. Spurning them as he passed he went down to the valleys, that the valleys might abound with grain.* The hills are thereafter condemned to an endless dryness and barrenness, as you may take the curse of the prophet: 'Let no dew or rain fall on you.'* And to bring home to you that these words were addressed to the angels who had stayed under the image of the mountains of Gilboa, he says: 'where many wounded have fallen'.* How many of the army of Israel have fallen in these accursed mountains from the beginning, and fall day by day! The same prophet refers to these when he says to God: 'Like the slain that lie in the grave, like those whom you remember no more, for they are cut off from your hand.'*

3. No wonder then if what are but airy hills rather than heavenly mountains remain barren and fruitless, for neither dew nor rain falls on them. He who is the source of grace and profuse blessings bounds over them and goes down to the valleys, to drench with heavenly showers the humble who live on

Ps 96:5

Ps 64:14

2 Sam 1:21

2 Sam 1:18-19

Ps 87:6

earth, that they may bring forth fruit with patience,* 'some a hundredfold, some sixty, some thirty'.* And there he visited the earth and saturated it, and multiplied its riches.* He visited the earth, not the air, since 'the earth is full of the mercy of the Lord'.* There he brought about salvation throughout the earth'.* Did he also do it up in the air? Here I oppose Origen, who by an impudent lie crucified the Lord of glory* again in the air for the redemption of the devils;[1] whereas St Paul, the confidant of this mystery, affirms that 'being raised from the dead he will never die again; death no longer has dominion over him'.*

*Lk 8:15
*Mt 13:8 & 23
*Ps 64:10
*Ps 32:5
*Ps 73:12
*1 Cor 2:8
*Rom 6:9

4. Actually he who bounded over the air visited not only the earth but also heaven, for Scripture says: 'Your love, O Lord, reaches up to heaven, your faithfulness to the clouds.'* Heaven up to the clouds is where the holy angels dwell: over these the Lord does not bound, but so leaps in them that he impresses on them the prints of his two feet, his mercy and his truth; I recall having discoursed fully on these footprints of the Lord in previous sermons.* But, from the clouds downward, in the foul and darksome air, is the dwelling-place of the devils. The bridegroom does not leap in these, he bounds over them and goes by, so that they retain no imprint of God's passage. How can the devil possess truth?

*Ps 35:6
*Sermon 6:6-9
(CF 4:35-7)

1. Modern scholars think that Origen's interpretation of the *apocata-stasis*, or final restoration and unity of all things, was not heretical. 'No precise text of his holds the salvation of the devil.' *New Catholic Encyclopaedia*, Vol X, p. 772, col. I. Cf. *Sacramentum Mundi*, I:51.

Truth's statement about him in the Gospels is clear: 'he does not stand in the truth', but is a liar from the beginning.* Neither will anyone call him merciful who is convinced by the very same gospel truth that he was a murderer from the beginning. Furthermore, as the master of the house is, so are the members of his household.* Hence the Church so excellently sings of her bridegroom that he dwells in the heights and cares for the lowly in heaven and on earth;* she makes no mention of those proud spirits who live in the air, because 'God opposes the proud but gives grace to the humble'.*

*Jn 8:44

*Mt 10:25

*Ps 112:5-6

*Jas 4:6

5. She sees him then, leaping on the mountains, bounding over the hills, in accord with that curse of David which says: Let the Lord visit all the mountains round about it— that is, round Gilboa—but let him pass by Gilboa.* There are mountains which the Lord visits on two sides of this Gilboa which designates the devil: angels above, men below.

*Responsory 4, Nocturn I, Vigils of Sundays after Pentecost. Cf. 2 Sam 1:21.

III. As he fell from heaven he was alotted for punishment that place in the air midway between heaven and earth,* where he might see sights to envy and be tormented by that envy, according to Scripture: 'The wicked man sees and is angry; he gnashes his teeth and consumes away'.* How wretched [he is] when he looks up to heaven and sees the countless mountains shining with a divine brightness, echoing with the divine praises, excelling in glory, abounding in grace! More wretched still when he looks to the earth that also possesses so many mountains of the

*Eph 2:2

*Ps 111:10

people claimed by God, solid in faith, ennobled by hope, enlarged by love, accomplished in virtues, laden with the fruit of good works, and gathering a daily blessing from the dew of heaven,* even the leaping of the bridegroom! Let us consider with what great remorse and spite he gazes on those splendid mountains all about him, ravenous for glory, while he despises himself and his followers as utterly uncouth, benighted, fruitless in every good, aware that he, who taunted everybody, is scorned by men and angels; as the psalm says: 'here is the dragon whom you have made your plaything.'*

6.   All this because the bridegroom bounds over them in their pride, leaping amid the mountains round about him like the fountain welling up in the midst of paradise,* irrigating all things and filling every animal with blessing.* Happy those who sometimes, even if rarely, deserve to drink from this fountain of delight. And even if it fails to flow in them continually, at least there are times when the water of wisdom,* the fountain of life,† leaps up, that it may become in them too a fountain of water 'welling up to eternal life'.* Yes, the onrush of this river refreshes the city of God perennially and abundantly.* How I wish that it would inundate our mountains here on earth from time to time, that he would sometimes condescend to leap on them, so that thus irrigated they might distil even rare droplets on us valleys, lest we remain entirely dry and barren. Misery and indigence and deadly famine prevail in that region* which is never moistened by those

Gen 27:28

Ps 103:26

Gen 2:6

Ps 144:16

Sir 15:3
†Ps 35:10

Jn 4:14

Ps 45:5

Lk 15:14

leapings and sprinklings, as the fountain of wisdom abounds over it and flows by: 'Because they lack wisdom', it says, 'they perished for their own folly.'*

    *Bar 3:28

7. 'See how he comes, leaping upon the mountains, bounding over the hills.'* He leaps in order to overleap, for he has no wish to extend himself to all: many of them did not please God.*

    *Sg 2:8

    *1 Cor 10:5

IV. Brothers, if, as Paul in his wisdom says, these · things 'were written down for our instruction',* let us observe the discreet and circumspect leapings of the bridegroom, how, both among angels and ourselves, he leaps among the humble and bounds over the proud; 'for though the Lord is high he has respect for the lowly, but the haughty he recognizes from afar.'* Let us attend to this so as to make sure we prepare ourselves for the redemptive leapings of the bridegroom, for fear that if he perceives us to be unworthy of his visitation, he may also pass us by like the mountains of Gilboa. What are you proud of, dust and ashes?* The Lord overleaped even the angels, abominating their pride. Let this rejection of the angels result in man's correction, for this was recorded for his instruction. Let even the wickedness of the devil contribute to my good,* let me wash my hands in the blood of the sinner.* How? you ask. Listen. A terrible and fear-inspiring curse is hurled at the proud devil by the prophet David, speaking in the spirit, who says under the figure of Gilboa, as previously noted:* Let the Lord visit all the mountains

    *1 Cor 10:11

    *Ps 137:6

    *Sir 10:9

    *Rom 8:28
    *Ps 57:11

    * ¶5 above

round about, but let him pass by Gilboa.

8. And indeed when I read this and turn my eyes on myself and look very carefully, I find myself infected by that pestilence which the Lord so abhorred in the angel that he shunned him because of it, while he honored with the favor of his visitation all the mountains round about, whether of angels or of men. So in fear and trembling I say to myself: 'If this is what happened to an angel, what will happen to me, to dust and ashes? He got puffed up in heaven, I on a dung-heap. Does anyone not see that pride is more tolerable in the rich than in the poor? Woe to me! If one so powerful was chastised so harshly because his heart was inflated, and the pride so congenial to the powerful availed him nothing, what will be demanded of me, so despicable in my pride? Even now I pay the penalty. I am bitterly flogged. It is not without reason that this languor of soul, this dullness of mind has laid hold of me since yesterday and the day before, an unwonted impotence of the spirit. I was running well;* but there in the way was the stumbling block:* I tripped and fell. Pride was discovered in me, and the Lord has turned away in anger from his servant.* Hence the barrenness of my spirit and the resourcelessness of devotion that I suffer. How has my heart withered* like this, congealed like milk,† become like land without water?* That sorrow from which tears spring I cannot find, such is my heart's hardness.* The psalms are stale, reading is disagreeable, prayer is devoid of joy, the accustomed meditations irretriev-

*Gal 5:7

*Rom 9:32

*Ps 26:9

*Jb 6:2
†Ps 118:70
*Ps 142:6

*Mk 16:14

able. Where now that intoxication of the
Spirit?* Where that serenity of mind, and
peace, and joy in the Holy Spirit?* This is
the reason for repugnance for work, drowsi-
ness at vigils, quickness to anger, obduracy in
hatred, over-indulgence of tongue and appe-
tite, greater indifference and dullness in
preaching. Alas! The Lord visits all the
mountains round about me, but me he does
not approach. Am I one of those hills over
which the bridegroom bounds? For I observe
that someone else stands out for abstinence,
another for admirable patience, still another
for perfect humility and meekness, yet another for great mercy and devotion; this
person is often rapt in contemplation, that
one knocks at and penetrates the heavens by
the urgency of his prayer,* still others excell
in other virtues. All of these, I repeat, I consider to be fervent, all of them prayerful, all of
one mind in Christ, all enriched with grace
and heavenly gifts, like real spiritual mountains that are visited by the Lord, that frequently welcome the bridegroom as he leaps
among them. But I, who find within me none
of these things, how else shall I regard myself
than as one of the mountains of Gilboa, whom
the kindest of all visitors passes by in his
anger and indignation?'

9. Dear sons, this thought puts an end to
haughtiness of the eyes,* attracts grace, pre-
pares for the leapings of the bridegroom. I
have applied these things to myself for your
sake, that you may do likewise.* Be my
imitators.† I am not talking now of the
practice of virtues, or disciplined behavior, or

Eph 5:18
Rom 14:17

Sir 35:17

Sir 23:5

1 Cor 4:6
†*Phil 3:17*

the glory of holiness: for I would not rashly claim in myself any of these gifts worthy of imitation. But I want you not to spare yourselves, but to accuse yourselves as often as you discern, even slightly, that grace is getting lukewarm, that virtue is languishing, even as I, too, accuse myself of such things. This is how a man acts who cautiously assesses himself, who examines his tendencies and desires and in everything watches relentlessly for the vice of arrogance, lest it take him by stealth. In very truth, I have learned nothing is so efficacious for the gaining, the retention, and the recovery of grace as to discover that in God's presence you must always stand in awe rather than yield to pride.* 'Blessed is the man who is always fearful.'* Fear therefore when grace smiles on you, fear when it departs, fear when it returns again; this is to be fearful always. These three fears succeed each other, one after another, in the soul, according as grace is sensed as gently present, as withdrawing when offended, or as coming back appeased. When it is present, fear lest your actions be unworthy of it. Now the apostle warns us, saying: See to it you do not receive the grace of God in vain'.* To his disciple he said: 'Do not neglect the grace that is in you';* and concerning himself he said: 'God's grace to me was not in vain.'* This man, confidant of God's plans, knew that to neglect a gift, not to use it for its intended purpose, would redound to contempt for the giver, and he considered it intolerable pride. So he himself zealously guarded against this evil and instructed others to beware of it. But yet

*Rom 11:20
*Prov 28:14

*2 Cor 6:1
*1 Tim 4:14

*1 Cor 15:10

another pitfall is hidden here that I must uncover for you, because, as you have in the
psalm: the spirit of pride himself lurks there
like a lion in his den,* all the more danger-   *Ps 9:30
ous as it is the more concealed. For if he fails
to prevent the action he attacks the intention, suggesting and wheedling how you may
ascribe to yourself the effect of grace. Have
no doubt that this kind of pride is more
intolerable by far than the other. For what
is more hateful than the voice in which some
have said: 'It was our triumphant hand, and
not the Lord, that performed all these
things'?*   *Deut 32:27

10. So then we must fear when grace is
present. What if it departs? Must we not then
fear much more? Obviously much more,
because when grace fails you, you fail. Just
listen to what the giver of grace says: 'without
me you can do nothing.'* Fear, therefore,   *Jn 15:5
when grace is withdrawn, like a man who is
liable to fall. Fear and tremble, as you become
aware that God is angry with you. Fear,
because your keeper has abandoned you. Do
not doubt that pride is the cause, even if it
does not seem so, even though you are not
conscious of it. For God knows what you do
not know, and he is the one who judges you.*   *1 Cor 4:4
'It is not the man who commends himself who
is accepted, but the man whom the Lord
commends.'* Does God in any way commend   *2 Cor 10:18
you when he deprives you of grace? Is it
possible that he who gives grace to the
humble* takes his gift away from the hum-   *Jas 4:6
ble? Therefore the deprivation of grace is a
proof of pride. There are times though when it

is withdrawn, not because of pride already present, but because of pride that will occur unless it is withdrawn. You have clear evidence of this from the Apostle, who unwillingly endured the thorns of his flesh,* not because he was puffed up but lest he be puffed up. But whether already, or not yet existing, pride will always be a cause of the withdrawal of grace.

*2 Cor 12:7

11. Now if grace returns appeased one must then fear all the more lest he suffer a relapse, as that gospel text teaches: 'See, you are well, go and sin no more, that nothing worse befall you'.* You hear that a second fall is worse than the first. As the danger increases, then, let fear also increase. You are fortunate if you have filled your heart with that threefold fear: that you fear when grace is received, even more when it is lost, and far more when it is recovered. Do this and you will be a water jar at Christ's banquet, filled to the very brim, containing not two measures merely but three,* and so you shall win the blessing of Christ who will change your waters into the wine of gladness, and perfect love will banish fear.*

*Jn 5:14

*Jn 2:6-7

*1 Jn 4:18

12. What I mean is this. Fear is water, because it cools the heat of carnal desires. The fear of the Lord is the beginning of wisdom,'* it says, and again: 'she gave him the water of wisdom to drink.'* If fear is wisdom and wisdom is water, then fear is water. Hence, 'the fear of the Lord is a fountain of life.'* Moreover, your mind is a water jar. Each of them, scripture says, contain two or three measures.* Three measures, three

*Ps 110:10
*Sir 15:3

*Prov 14:27

*Jn 2:6

fears. 'And they filled them to the brim',* it
says. Not one fear, not even two, but all
three together fill the mind to the brim. Fear
the Lord at all times, and from your whole
heart, and you have filled the jar to the brim.
God loves an entire gift, a total affection,
a perfect sacrifice. Take care then to bring to
the heavenly nuptials a water jar that is full,
so that it may be said of you, too, 'the spirit
of the fear of the Lord filled him'.* He who
fears like this neglects nothing. For how can
negligence insinuate itself into fullness? In
any case something which still has room for
more is not full. For the same reason you
cannot possess this fear and at the same time
be puffed up.* Filled with the fear of the
Lord you have no means of entertaining
pride. And other vices must be similarly
judged, all are of necessity excluded by the
fullness of fear. Then at last, if your fear is
full and perfect, love, at the blessing of the
Lord, will add flavor to your waters. For
without love fear expects punishment.* Love
is the wine that gladdens man's heart.*
'Perfect love casts out fear',* and what was
water becomes wine, to the praise and glory
of the Church's bridegroom, our Lord Jesus
Christ, who is above all things God, blessed
for ever.* Amen.

*Jn 2:7

*Is 11:3

*Rom 11:20

*1 Jn 4:18
*Ps 103:15
*1 Jn 4:18

*Rom 9:5

SERMON FIFTY-FIVE

I. WHY THE BRIDEGROOM IS COMPARED
TO A GAZELLE OR A FAWN.   II. HOW
WE OUGHT TO JUDGE OURSELVES, LEST
WE BE JUDGED.

*Sg 2:9

I. 1. '**M**Y BELOVED IS LIKE A GA-
ZELLE, or a fawn.'* This refers
to the preceding verse. She has
just described him as leaping and bounding,
so now she compares him to a gazelle or a
fawn. Aptly, indeed, because this breed of
animals leaps nimbly and runs swiftly. Besides,
the word concerns the bridegroom, and the
bridegroom is the Word.* And the prophet
says of God that 'his word runs swiftly',*
which fits into this context where the bridegroom, who is the Word of God, is described
as leaping and bounding, and therefore resem-
bling the gazelle and the fawn. This is the reason for the comparison. But lest any element,
even the tiniest, be lacking to the comparison,
remember that the gazelle excels not only in
fleetness of foot but also in sharpness of sight.
This refers to that part of the narrative in
which the bridegroom is described as seeming
not only to leap but to bound over, because
only by sharp and penetrating sight would
it be at all possible, especially in running, to

*Sermo
*Ps 147:15

discern where he ought to leap and over what to bound. Otherwise, a comparison with the fawn alone would have sufficed to designate the swiftness of the runner, for he is known to move with the swiftest speed. But now, while this bridegroom, in the ardor of his love, seems to rush eagerly into the embraces of the beloved, he nevertheless knows how to direct his steps, or rather his leapings, with prudent consideration, being wary as to where to place his foot. A comparison with the gazelle as well as with the fawn is therefore called for, since the latter expresses the desire to save and the former the decision to choose. Christ is righteous and merciful,* of course, a saviour and a judge. Because he loves he wills that all men be saved and come to a knowledge of the truth,* and because he judges he knows who are his, he knows whom he has chosen from the beginning.*

2. Meanwhile therefore let us be aware that these two gifts, mercy and judgment, are commended to us by the Holy Spirit in those two animals, so that in witnessing to the integrity and perfection of our faith, we too may imitate the prophet and sing of mercy and judgment to the Lord.* I have no doubt that those who are inquisitive and well-informed about such things can point to other qualities of these animals that may profitably and suitably be applied to the bridegroom; but these are enough, I think, to explain the given comparison. But how beautiful that the Holy Spirit drew the comparison not from the stag but from the fawn. By it he calls to mind both the Fathers who are Christ's

*Cf. 2 Mac 1:24

*1 Tim 2:4

*Jn 13:18

*Ps 100:1

*Rom 9:5

*Is 9:6

*Zeph 1:12

*Ps 7:10
*Ps 75:11

*1 Tim 5:24

*Ps 74:3

ancestors according to the flesh,* and the Saviour's infancy. For the child who was born to us* appeared as a fawn. But you who long for the advent of the Saviour are afraid of the Judge's scrutiny, afraid of the eyes of the gazelle, afraid of him who says by the prophet: 'On that day I will search Jerusalem with lamps.'* His sight is sharp: his eye will leave nothing unexplored. He will scrutinize minds and hearts,* man's very thought will open up to him.* If Jerusalem is to be scrutinized, what is safe in Babylon? For I think that in this passage the prophet indicates by the name Jerusalem those who lead a religious life in this world, imitating as far as they can the ways of the heavenly Jerusalem by an upright and orderly life-style, and do not, like the citizens of Babylon, waste their life in a chaos of vices and the turmoil of crimes. Their sins are obvious,* going before them to the judgment. They do not need to be scrutinized but to throw themselves on his mercy. But I, a monk and a Jerusalemite, have sins that are definitely hidden, overshadowed by the name and habit of a monk; and consequently it is necessary to probe them with an exacting investigation, and bring them from darkness to light, as it were by the aid of lamps.

II. 3. We can quote also from the psalm to confirm what has been said about the examining of Jerusalem. It says in the person of the Lord: 'when I have set the time, I—justice—will judge.'* Unless I am mistaken, he says he will discuss and examine the ways and actions of the just. We must be very much afraid

that, when that time comes, under so exacting
a scrutiny much of our righteousness may
show up as sin. There is only one thing to do:
if we shall have judged ourselves we shall not
be judged.* How good the judgment that   *1 Cor 11:31*
withdraws me and hides me from the strict
judgment of God. I am utterly terrified of
falling into the hands of the living God;* I   *Heb 10:31*
prefer to be presented before his angry face
judged rather than to-be-judged. 'The spiritual
man judges all things, but is himself judged by
no one.'* I shall judge my evil deeds, there-   *1 Cor 2:15*
fore I shall judge even my good deeds. I shall
strive to correct the evils by better conduct,
to wash them away with tears, to chastise
them with fastings and other exercises of the
holy discipline. Where good is concerned I
shall think humbly of myself and, in accord
with the Lord's commandment, regard myself as a useless servant who did no more than
I was bound to do.* I shall endeavour not to   *Lk 17:10*
offer cockle for grain,* nor chaff with the   *Mt 13:25-30*
grain. I shall scrutinize my habits and pursuits,
so that he who will examine Jerusalem with
lamps may find nothing in me unexamined or
untested. For he will not judge the same
thing twice.

4. Who will enable me to search out
thoroughly and punish all my sins, that I may
have no reason to fear the eyes of the gazelle,
have no cause to blush in the light of the
lamps? Now I am seen, but I do not see. The
eye is present to which all things are visible,
though which is itself invisible. A time will
come when I shall know even as I am
known.* But now I know in part, though I am   *1 Cor 13:12*

known not partially but totally. I am afraid of the appearance of that watcher who stands behind the wall. Scripture adds the following about him whom it compares to a gazelle for his sharpness of sight: 'Behold, there he stands behind our wall, gazing in at the windows, looking through the lattice.'* We shall look at this in its place.* And so I fear this hidden watcher of hidden things. The bride fears nothing, because she is not aware of anything against herself.* What should she, his friend, his dove, his beautiful one, be afraid of? Further on you read: 'And my beloved speaks to me.'* He does not speak to me, and therefore I dread his appearance, because I lack credentials. You, his bride, what do you hear about yourself? What does your beloved say to you? 'Arise,' he says, 'make haste, my love, my dove, my beautiful one.'* But this too I shall reserve for another sermon.* I will not compress too briefly things that demand industrious care, lest I be burdened with further guilt if you do not find yourselves built up in the knowledge and love of the Church's bridegroom, our Lord Jesus Christ, who is God over all things, blessed for ever.* Amen.

*Sg 2:9
*Sermon 56

*1 Cor 4:4

*Sg 2:10

*Ibid.
*Sermon 57

*Rom 9:5

SERMON FIFTY-SIX

I. WHAT IS THE WALL, WHAT ARE THE
WINDOWS OR CHINKS THROUGH WHICH
THE BRIDEGROOM LOOKS? II. HOW
HE IS BEHIND THE WALL FOR EACH OF
US; HIS PRESENCE AND HIS ABSENCE.
III. HOW SOME ERECT MANY WALLS BE-
TWEEN THEMSELVES AND THE BRIDE-
GROOM, AND THE MORAL OF THE LAT-
TICES AND WINDOWS.

I. 1. 'BEHOLD, THERE HE STANDS behind our wall, gazing in at the windows, looking through the lattices.'* As the words stand, they seem to say that he who was seen coming by leaps and bounds has arrived at the Bride's dwelling and, standing behind the wall, peeps inquisitively through the windows and chinks, because he is too modest to presume to enter. According to the spiritual meaning, however, he is understood to have drawn near, but in a different way, as it befits the heavenly Bridegroom to behave and the Holy Spirit to describe it. A true spiritual understanding will not condone what ill becomes either the one who acts or the one who describes the action. He drew near the wall, therefore, when he joined himself to our flesh. Our flesh is the

*Sg 2:9

87

wall, and the Bridegroom's approach is the incarnation of the Word. The windows and lattices through which he is said to gaze can be understood, I think, as the bodily senses and human feelings by which he began to experience all our human needs. For 'he has borne our griefs and carried our sorrows'.* On being made man, therefore, he has used our bodily feelings and senses as openings or windows, so that he would know by experience the miseries of men and might become merciful.* These were things he already knew but in a different way. As Lord of the virtues he knew the virtue of obedience, and yet the apostle bears witness that 'he learned obedience through what he suffered'.* By this means he also learned mercy, although the mercy of the Lord is from eternity.* This same teacher of the Gentiles teaches this again when he states that He was tempted in all things as we are without sin, in order to become merciful.* Do you see him becoming what he [already] was, and learning what he [already] knew, seeking in our midst openings and windows by which to search more attentively into our misfortunes? He found as many openings in our tumbling down and fissured wall as he experienced proofs of our weakness and corruption in his own body.

2. This then is how the Bridegroom stands behind the wall and looks through the windows and lattices. 'Stands' is the right word, because he alone who never experienced the sin of the flesh, truly stood in the flesh. This we can duly discern, because he who sank down through the weakness of the flesh stood

*Is 53:4

*Heb 2:17

*Heb 5:8

*Ps 102:17

*Heb 4:15

erect by the power of divinity, as he said
himself: 'The spirit indeed is willing but the
flesh is weak.'* I think too that this interpretation is supported by what David said of
Christ with regard to this mystery; for he
prophesied as the Lord's prophet, and though
speaking of Moses was contemplating Christ.
For [Christ] is the true Moses who came
indeed by water, though 'not by water only
but by water and blood'.* Hence the fore-
mentioned prophet says, referring to God the
Father: 'He said he would destroy them, had
not Moses his chosen one stood in the breach
before his gaze, to turn away his wrath lest
He destroy them.'* How, I ask, did Moses
stand in the breach? How, I repeat, could he
stand if he were broken down or, if he stood,
how could he have been broken down?[1] But
I'll let you see, if you wish, who really stood
in the breach. I know of no one else who
could achieve this except my Lord Jesus, who
certainly lived in death, who while broken in
body on the cross stood erect with the Father
in his divinity: petitioning with us in the one,
appeasing the Father in the other. His standing behind the wall then means that his
prostrate weakness was revealed in the flesh,
while that which stood erect in him was hidden by the flesh: the man revealed and the
hidden God* are one and the same.

*Mt 26:41

*1 Jn 5:6

*Ps 105:23

*Is 45:15

II. 3. And for each one of us who desire his

---

1. This passage is not clear. St Bernard seems to impose a reflexive
meaning on the text to accommodate the point he wants to make
about Christ.

coming he also stands behind the wall as long as this body of ours, which is certainly sinful,* hides his face from us and shuts out his presence. For 'so long as we are in this body we are exiles from the Lord'.* Not because we are embodied, but because we are in this body which has a sinful lineage, and is never without sin. So you may know that it is not our bodies but our sins that stand in the way, listen to what Scripture says: 'it is our sins that raise a barrier between us and God.'* How I wish that the body's wall were the only obstacle, that I should suffer only that single barrier of fleshly sin and not the many fences of vice that intervene! I am afraid that through my own weakness I have added a host of sins to that which my nature inherits, and by them I set the Bridegroom at too great a distance from me, so that if I am to speak the truth I must confess that to me he stands not behind a wall but behind walls.

4. Let me say it more plainly. Through the immediacy of his divine majesty and the greatness of his power the Bridegroom is present, equally and without distinction, in every place.* But with regard to rational creatures, angels and men, he is said to be near to some and far from others by holding out or withholding grace. For 'salvation is far from the wicked'.* And yet the holy man says: 'why do you stand so far off, Lord?'* Indeed he sometimes, by a loving arrangement, withdraws far from his saints for a time, not entirely but in part. From sinners, however, he is always very far removed, and that in anger, not in mercy. Of them it is said:

*Rom 6:6

*2 Cor 5:6

*Is 59:2

*Eph 1:19

*Ps 118:155
*Ps 9:22

'Their pride rises up continually';* and again: *Ps 73:23
'his ways are filthy at all times.'* Hence the *Ps 9:26
holy man prays to the Lord and says: 'Turn
not away in anger from your servant,'* *Ps 26:9
knowing that he can also turn away in mercy.
And so the Lord is close to his saints and
chosen ones even when he seems far away,
though not at an equal distance from all, but
farther from some, less far from others
according to their varying merits. Although
the Lord is near to all who call upon him in
truth,* and though he is near to the broken- *Ps 144:18
hearted,* he is not perhaps so close to all that *Ps 33:19
they can say he stands behind the wall. Yet
how close he is to the bride who is separated
by one wall only! On this account she longs
that the dividing wall be broken down, that
she may die and be with him who,* she trusts, *Phil 1:23
is behind the wall.

5. But I, because I am a sinful man,* have *Lk 5:8
no wish to be dissolved. Instead I am afraid,
knowing that the death of the wicked is very
evil.* How can death not be very evil where *Ps 33:22
Life brings no help? I am afraid to go forth.
I tremble at the very entrance of the haven,
because I have no assurance that he is standing by to receive me at my exit. And why?
Do I go forth securely if the Lord does not
guard my going forth?* Alas! Unless he who *Ps 120:8
redeems and saves is standing by* I shall be *Ps 7:3
the laughing-stock of the devils who inter-
cept me. Nothing like this troubled the soul
of Paul, whom one wall only separated from
the vision and embrace of his beloved, that is,
the law of sin that he discovered in his members.* This is that sensuality of the *Rom 7:23

*1 Jn 2:16

*Rom 7:24

*1 Cor 4:4

*Rom 6:16

*Prov 18:3

*Sir 51:4

body* that he could not possibly avoid while living on earth. But despite the obtrusion of this wall he did not wander far from the Lord. Therefore he cried out longingly: 'who will deliver me from this body of death?'* He knew that by the short passage of death he would at once attain life. So Paul averred that he was in bonds to this one law, sensual desire, which he unwillingly endured because it was rooted in his flesh. As for the rest he could say: 'I am not aware of anything against myself.'*

III. 6. But is there anyone like Paul, anyone who does not consent at times to this sensual desire and so submits to sin?* Let him who yields to sin take note that he has raised another wall against himself by that wicked and unlawful consent. A man of this kind cannot boast that for him the Bridegroom stands behind the wall, because not one wall but walls now intervene. Much less still if the consent has passed into action, for then a third wall, the sinful act itself, wards off and bars the Bridegroom's approach. But what if the repetition of sins becomes a habit, or the habit induces contempt, as Scripture says: 'When wickedness comes, contempt comes also'?* If you die like this, will you not be devoured a thousand times by those that roar as they await their food,* before you can reach the Bridegroom now shut off from you not merely by one, but by a succession of walls? The first is sensual desire; the second, consent; the third, the action; the fourth, habit; the fifth, contempt. Take care then to resist with

all your strength the first movements of
sensual desire lest they lure you to consent,
and then the whole fabric of wickedness will
vanish. Then there will be but the wall of the
body to hinder the Bridegroom's approach to
you, so that you may proclaim with gladness:
'behold, there he stands behind our wall.'*   **Sg 2:9*

7. But there is one thing you must attend
to with total vigilance: that you always open
the windows and lattices of your confessions.
Through them his kindly gaze may penetrate
to your inward life, because his discerning is
your learning. They say that lattices* are   **cancelli*
narrow windows, similar to what writers of
books provide for themselves to direct light
on to the page. I think this is why those whose
work is the drawing up of official documents
are called chancellors.* Since therefore there   **cancellarii*
are two kinds of compunction—the one in
sorrow for our deviations, the other in rejoicing for God's gifts—as often as I make that
confession of my sins which is always accom-
panied by anguish of heart,* I seem to open   **2 Cor 2:4*
for myself a lattice or narrow window. Nor
do I doubt that the devoted examiner who
stands behind the wall looks through it
with pleasure, because God will not despise a
humble and contrite heart.* One is even ex-   **Ps 50:19*
horted to do this: confess your iniquities
that you may be made righteous.* But if at   **Is 43:26*
times, when the heart expands in love at the
thought of God's graciousness and mercy, it
is all right to surrender our mind, to let
it go in songs of praise and gratitude, I
feel that I have opened up to the Bridegroom
who stands behind the wall not a narrow

lattice but a wide-open window. Through it, unless I am mistaken, he will look in with greater pleasure the more he is honored by the sacrifice of praise.* I can easily show from Scripture that he approves of both these confessions; but I am speaking to those who are aware of this,* and I must not burden with superfluities men whose time scarce suffices to pursue the essentials: the great mysteries of this love-song and the praises it proclaims to the Church and her Bridegroom, Jesus Christ our Lord, who is God over all, blessed for ever.* Amen.

*Ps 49:23

*Rom 7:1

*Rom 9:5

SERMON FIFTY-SEVEN

I. THE LEVELS OF GOD'S GRACIOUSNESS
OR CONTEMPLATION OF HIM ACCORDING
AS HE GRANTS FEAR TO SOME, SECURITY
TO OTHERS.   II. EACH ONE OUGHT TO
WATCH FOR THE COMING OF THE BRIDE-
GROOM;   THE   TESTIMONIES   OF   GOD.
III. THE LEVELS BY WHICH THE SOUL
WEIGHS   UP   THE   BRIDEGROOM'S   AP-
PROACH   OR   COMING.   IV. THE INTER-
CHANGE OF CHASTE CONTEMPLATION;
HOW LOVER, DOVE AND BEAUTIFUL ONE
DIFFER,   IN   MARY,   LAZARUS   AND
MARTHA.

I. 1. '**M**Y BELOVED SPEAKS TO ME.' *Sg 2:10
Look at the ways of grace, take
note of the levels of God's
graciousness. Study the devotion and sagacity
of the bride, with what a vigilant eye she
watches for the bridegroom's coming and
scrutinizes everything about him. He comes,
he comes faster, he draws near, he is here, he
looks about, he speaks, and not one of these
details escapes the diligence or the alertness
of the waiting bride. He comes in the angels,
he comes faster in the patriarchs, draws near
in the prophets, is here in the incarnation,
looks about in his miracles, speaks in his

apostles. Or again: he comes with love and desire to show mercy, he comes faster in his eagerness to help, he draws near by assuming our lowliness,* he is here to his contemporaries, looks ahead to future generations, speaks by teaching and convincing men of the kingdom of God.* Such is the Bridegroom's coming. The joys and gifts of salvation come with him,* everything about him exudes delight, redounds with delectable and health-giving mysteries. And she who loves keeps vigil, and watches all this. Happy for her that the Lord finds her watching.* He will not pass her by or ignore her, he will stand and speak to her. He will speak words of love, he will speak, indeed, as the beloved. So you have [the text]: And my beloved speaks to me.* Well beloved, he comes to speak words of love, not of reproach.

2. Nor is she one of those who are rightly blamed by the Lord for not knowing how to judge the look of the sky while being unaware of the time of his coming.* So sagacious is she, so experienced, so keenly vigilant, that she spied him coming a long way off, she heeded him leaping as he sped along, bounding over the proud,* that through lowliness he might draw near to her lowly person. This she observed with the utmost watchfulness. And when he finally stopped and hid behind the wall she nevertheless recognized his presence and was acutely aware that he was looking through the windows and lattices. Now as a reward for her great devotion and holy excitement, she hears him speak. If he had looked and had not spoken she could have suspected

*Phil 2:8

*Acts 19:8

*Is 33:6

*Lk 12:37

*Sg 2:10

*Mt 16:3

*Sg 2:8

that this look implied censure rather than love. He looked at Peter, without saying a word; perhaps he wept because He remained silent when He looked.* But she, because he addressed her after looking, not only does not weep but cries out with happiness and boasts: 'my beloved speaks to me.' You see, the gaze of the Lord, though ever in itself unchanged, does not always produce the same effect. It conforms to each person's deserts, inspiring some with fear but bringing solace and security to others. For 'he looks on the earth and it trembles',* whereas he looks on Mary and fills her with grace. 'He has looked upon his lowly handmaid,' she said, 'and from this day forward all generations will call me blessed.'* These are the words of a happy girl, not of one who weeps in dread. In like manner he looks at the bride, but she does not tremble or weep like Peter,* for unlike him she is not earthly-minded.* Instead he filled her heart with joy,* revealing by his words the affection with which he looked at her.   3. Hear then the words he speaks, words surely of a lover, not of a censurer.

*Lk 22:61-62

*Ps 103:32

*Lk 1:48

*Lk 22:62
*Phil 3:19
*Ps 4:7

II. He says: 'Arise, make haste, my love, my dove, my beautiful one.'* Happy the conscience which deserves to hear these words! Who among us, do you think, is so vigilant, so attentive to the time of his visitation and the Bridegroom's coming that he every moment scans every detail of his approach, so that when He comes and knocks, he opens the door to Him right away?* These words are not so applied to the Church as to exclude

*Sg 2:10

*Lk 12:36

any one of us, who together are the Church, from a share in its blessings. For in this respect we are all, universally and without distinction, called to possess the blessings as our heritage.* Hence [the psalmist] dared to say to the Lord: 'Your testimonies are my eternal heritage, they are the joy of my heart,'* a heritage, I think, by which he saw himself as a son of the Father who is in heaven.* For if a son then an heir, an heir of God and a fellow heir with Christ.* And he boasts that in this heritage he has acquired a great boon: the testimonies of the Lord. Would that I deserved to possess even one testimony of the Lord about myself, because [the psalmist] is glorying not in one but in many testimonies! He even says somewhere else: 'I delight in the way of your testimonies as much as in all riches.'* And indeed what are the riches of salvation,* what are the delights of the heart, what is the true and safe security of the mind except the attestations of the Lord? 'It is not the man who commends himself that is accepted', [the apostle] says, 'but the man whom the Lord commends.'*

4. Why do we continue to defraud ourselves of these divine commendations or testimonies, and deprive ourselves of our paternal heritage? We fail to recall that he has in any way commended us, or that he has uttered any testimony in our favor, as if he had not voluntarily made us his children by the word of truth.* What of what the apostle said, that the Spirit himself bears witness with our spirit that we are sons of God?* How are we

*1 Pet 3:9

*Ps 118:111

*Mt 7:21
*Rom 8:17

*Ps 118:14
*Is 33:6

*2 Cor 10:18

*Jas 1:18

*Rom 8:16

sons if deprived of the inheritance? Our very
impoverishment surely convicts us of negligence and indifference. For if any one of us,
following the wise man's word, sets his heart
fully and perfectly to rise early to seek the
Lord who made him, and pleads in the pre-
sence of the Most High,* if he strives at the   *Sir 39:6
same time with all diligence, following the
prophet Isaiah's advice, to prepare the ways
of the Lord, to make straight the paths of our
God,* if he can say with the psalmist: 'My   *Is 40:3
eyes are ever on the Lord',* and 'I keep the   *Ps 24:15
Lord always before me',* shall that person
not receive a blessing from the Lord and
mercy from God his saviour?* He will be   *Ps 23:5
visited often, and never be unaware of the
time of the visit,* even though he who visits   *Lk 19:44
in spirit comes secretly and stealthily like a
shy lover. The sober-minded soul who keeps
careful watch will see him coming a long way
off* and will discover everything that we have   *Lk 14:32
shown the bride taking note of so cleverly and
and so clearly in the approach of her beloved,
for he said: 'Those who seek me eagerly shall
find me.'* She will perceive the desire of the   *Prov 8:17
hastening [lover], and will immediately be
aware when he is near, and when actually
present. She will detect with happy eyes the
eye that gazes on her like a sun-ray piercing
through the windows and lattices of the
wall,* and at last she will hear the voices of   *Sg 2:9
jubilation and in love will call out: 'my love,
my dove, my beautiful one.'

III. 5. 'Shall the wise understand these
words',* that he may rightly distinguish and   *Hos 14:10

mark off each from the other, and explain them in a way that men will be able to grasp? If you expect this from me I should prefer you to hear it from an adept, from one accustomed to and experienced in these things. A person of this kind however chooses rather to hide in modest silence what he has perceived in silence, to keep his secret to himself as the safer course.* But as one bound in duty to speak, one who may not be silent, I relate to you whatever I know on this subject from my own or from others' experience. Since many can easily verify it, I leave deeper truths to those competent to comprehend them. If therefore I am warned, either outwardly by some person or inwardly by the Spirit, to maintain what is righteous and uphold what is reasonable, this wholesome counsel will be to me a presage of the Bridegroom's speedy coming, a preparation for the proper reception of the heavenly visitor. The prophet tells me this when he says: 'Righteousness will go before him';* or as he says to God: 'Righteousness and justice are the preparation of your throne'.* But a similar hope will gladden me if the discourse speaks of humility or patience, or of brotherly love and obedience to authority, but especially of the need to strive for holiness and peace and purity of heart, because Scripture says that 'holiness befits your house O Lord',* that 'his place is in peace',* and that 'the pure in heart shall see God'.* Whenever I am reminded of these or any other virtues, therefore, it will mean for me, as I said, that the Lord of virtues is about to visit my soul.

*Is 24:16

*Ps 84:14

*Ps 88:15

*Ps 92:5
*Ps 75:3
*Mt 5:8

6. Even if 'a good man strike or rebuke me in kindness'* I shall draw a similar inference, knowing that the zeal and benevolence of a good man make a pathway for him who ascends above the downfalling sun.† Happy that downfall when at the reproof of a good man his fellow is raised up and error is thrown down and the Lord ascends above it, treading it under foot to crush it lest it rise again. We must not therefore despise the good man's rebuke which destroys sin, gives healing to the heart and makes a path for God to the soul. No discourse whatsoever that promotes devotion or the virtues or moral perfection is to be heard with indifference, because that too is a way by which God's salvation is revealed.* And if the discourse sounds sweet and agreeable, if antipathy is banished by eagerness to listen, then not only is the Bridegroom believed to be on the way but to be speeding, that is, coming in one's desire. His desire gives rise to yours; and because you are eager to receive his word he is hastening to enter your heart; for he first loved us, not we him.* Moreover, if you listen to a fiery discourse and your conscience burns in a consequence at the memory of your sins, remember then what Scripture says of him: 'fire goes before him',* and be assured that he is near. In short, 'the Lord is close to those who are brokenhearted'.*

7. Yet if you are not only filled with sorrow by the discourse but totally converted to the Lord, vowing and determining to keep his just decrees,* you will know again that he is present, especially if you feel yourself aglow

*Ps 140:5

†Ps 67:5. *It is almost impossible to give a meaningful English rendering to Bernard's nuances on the word* occasum.

*Ps 49:23

*1 Jn 4:10

*Ps 96:3

*Ps 33:19

*Ps 118:106

with his love. These two things are written
of him—that fire goes before him and that he
himself is fire. For Moses said of him that he
is a devouring fire.* They differ, however,
because the fire that goes before has heat but
no love. It boils up but does not boil dry,
it moves but does not move forward. It is
sent on before only to arouse and prepare
you, to make you realize what you are of
yourself, that afterwards you may the more
sweetly relish what God's action makes of
you. The fire that is God does indeed devour
but it does not debase; it burns pleasantly,
devastates felicitously. It is a coal of deso-
lating fire,* but a fire that rages against vices
only to produce a healing unction in the
soul. Recognize therefore that the Lord is
present both in the power that transforms
you and in the love that sets you aglow. The
Lord's right hand has shown its power.* But
understand that this change from God's right
hand* takes place only in fervor of spirit and
genuine love.* Then you will be a man who
can say: 'My heart became hot within me, as I
mused the fire burned.'*

8. Furthermore, when this fire has con-
sumed every stain of sin and the rust of evil
habits, when the conscience has been cleansed
and tranquillized and there follows an immediate and unaccustomed expansion of the
mind, an infusion of light that illuminates the
intellect to understand Scripture and comprehend the mysteries—the first given for our
own satisfaction, the second for the instruction of our neighbors—all this undoubtedly
means that his eye beholds you, nurturing

*Dt 4:24

*Ps 119:4

*Ps 117:16

*Ps 76:11
*2 Cor 6:6

*Ps 38:4

your uprightness as a light and your integrity as the noonday,* as Isaiah says: 'Your light shall break forth as the dawn', etc.* But as long as this mere crumbling wall of the body stands this ray of intense brightness will pour itself in not through open doors but through chinks and crevices. You are wrong if you hope otherwise, no matter how great your purity of heart, because the greatest of contemplatives, Paul, says: 'Now we see only in a riddle and in a mirror, but then we shall see face to face.'*

*Ps 36:6
*Is 58:8

*1 Cor 13:12

9. After this glance, so full of graciousness and kindness, comes the soothing voice that gently insinuates God's will. It is no other than love itself, which cannot be idle, but invites and urges us along the ways of God. The bride too hears the call to arise and make haste, surely for the welfare of souls.

IV. It is characteristic of true and pure contemplation that when the mind is ardently aglow with God's love, it is sometimes so filled with zeal and the desire to gather to God those who will love him with equal abandon that it gladly foregoes contemplative leisure for the endeavor of preaching. And then, with its desire at least partially satisfied, it returns to its leisure with an eagerness proportionate to its successful interruption, until, refreshed again with the food of contemplation, it hastens to add to its conquests with renewed strength and experienced zeal. Quite often though the mind is tossed to and fro amid these changes, fearful and violently agitated lest it cling more than is justified to one or the other of these rival attractions and so deviate from God's will even momentarily. Perhaps holy Job endured this when he said: 'When I lie down I say, "when shall I arise?" And then I look forward to the evening.'* That is, when at prayer I accuse myself of indifference at work; when at work of upsetting my prayer. You see here a holy man violently tossed between the fruit of action and the quiet of contemplation:* through all the time involved in what is good he is ever repenting of imaginary sins, every moment seeking for the will of God with tears. For this man the only remedy, the last resort, is prayer and frequent appeals to God that He would deign to show us unceasingly what he wishes us to do, at what time, and in what measure. In the three words here designated and commended you have, I think, these three things: Preaching, prayer and contemplation. For she is fittingly addressed as his 'friend' who zealously and loyally works for the advantage of her Bridegroom by preaching, by counselling, by serving. Fittingly as his 'dove', for though she prays with sighing and supplication for her sins, she never fails to win the gift of mercy. Fittingly as his 'beautiful one', for though radiant with a longing for heaven, she clothes herself with the beauty of divine contemplation* only at those times when she may do so suitably and conveniently.

10. But see too whether these three endowments of the one soul may be related to those three persons living in one house, the Saviour's intimate friends.* I refer to Martha as serving, to Mary in repose, and to Lazarus

groaning beneath the stone, beseeching the grace of resurrection.* These remarks are based on the skill and vigilance with which the bride observes the ways of the Bridegroom, for the time and the speed of his coming to her cannot be hidden from her. No sudden intervention can distract her from knowing when he is far off, when he is near and when he is present, and so she deserves not only to be looked upon tenderly but to be gladdened by his words of love and 'to rejoice greatly at the Bridegroom's voice'.*

*Jn 11:39-44

*Jn 3:29

11. With a certain boldness I also maintain that the soul of any one of us here, if it keeps a similar vigil, will similarly be greeted as friend, consoled as the dove, embraced as a beauty. Each person shall be counted perfect in whom these three endowments shall be seen to unite in due order and degree, so that he will know how to mourn for his sins and to rejoice in God, and at the same time possess the power to assist his neighbors. He will please God, watch out for himself, and be of service to his friends. But who is up to all of these? Please God they may be preserved down the years among us all, if not all three in each one at least singly in different persons! For we discover Martha as the Saviour's friend in those who do the daily chores. We find Lazarus, the mourning dove,* in the novices just now dead to their sins,* who toil with fresh wounds and mourn through fear of the judgment. 'Like the slain that lie in the grave, like those you remember no more',* so they amount to nothing until Christ's command removes the burden of fear that crushes them

*Is 59:11
*1 Pet 2:24

*Ps 87:6

like a block of stone, and they can breathe again with the hope of pardon. We find a contemplative Mary in those who, co-operating with God's grace over a long period of time, have attained to a better and happier state. By now confident of forgiveness they no longer brood anxiously on the sad memory of their sins, but day and night they meditate on the ways of God with insatiable delight,* even at times gazing with unveiled face,* in unspeakable joy, on the splendor of the Bridegroom, being transformed into his likeness from splendor to splendor by the Spirit of the Lord. We shall examine in another sermon to what purpose he urges the bride to arise and make haste, he who shortly before had forbidden that she be aroused from sleep.* May he himself be with us, to reveal to us the meaning of this mystery, he the Church's Bridegroom, Jesus Christ our Lord, who is God over all things, blessed for ever.*

*Ps 1:2

*2 Cor 3:18

*Sg 2:7

*Rom 9:5

SERMON FIFTY-EIGHT

I. WHY THE BRIDE IS ORDERED TO
MAKE HASTE. II. THE SUITABLE TIME
FOR PRUNING, THE MEANING OF WINTER
AND THE FRUSTRATING RAIN. III.
THE GOOD AND EVIL CLOUDS AND
SHOWERS, AND THE FLOWERS THAT
AFTERWARDS APPEARED. IV. THE PRUN-
ING OF THE METAPHYSICAL VINE, THE
SOUL; WHEN THIS IS NECESSARY, WHICH
IS ALWAYS.

I. 1. 'ARISE, MAKE HASTE, my love, my dove, my beautiful one, and come.'* Who says this? Doubtless the Bridegroom. And is he not the one who, shortly before, earnestly forbade that his beloved be awakened? Why therefore does he now command her not only to arise but even to hurry? A similar incident from the Gospel comes to mind. On the very night on which the Lord was betrayed,* after he had ordered the disciples who were with him to sleep and take their rest, worn out as they were by prolonged watching, he immediately said to them: 'Rise, let us be going; see, my betrayer is at hand.'* Similarly here too, almost in the same instant he forbids that the bride be awakened, and then wakes her saying: 'Arise

*Sg 2:10

*1 Cor 11:23

*Mt 26:45,46

and come.' When can this sudden change of will or of plan mean? Are we to think that the Bridegroom is moved by caprice, first willing something and then rejecting it? Of course not. Rather you must acknowledge here those changes that I have previously and more than once explained to you concerning holy inactivity and essential action, how this life does not cater for constant contemplation or prolonged leisure, since we are impelled by the more cogent and more immediate demands of work and duty. When the Bridegroom therefore perceives, as he always does, that the bride has taken her rest for some time on his bosom, he does not hesitate to entice her out again to what seems more serviceable. It is not that she is unwilling, or that he himself is doing what he had forbidden. But if the bride is enticed by the Bridegroom this is because she receives from him the desire by which she is enticed, the desire of good works, the desire to bring forth fruit for the Bridegroom, for to her the Bridegroom is life, and death gain.*

*Phil 1:21

2. And that desire is vehement: it urges her not only to arise but to arise quickly for we read: 'Arise, make haste, and come.'* It is no small consolation to her that she hears 'come' and not 'go', knowing from this that she is being invited rather than sent, and that the Bridegroom will be coming with her. For what will she reckon difficult with him as her companion? 'Set me beside you', she says, 'and let any man's hand fight against me.'* Or: 'Even though I walk through the valley of the shadow of death, I fear no evil for you are

*Sg 2:10

*Jb 17:3

with me.'* She is not therefore aroused   *Ps 22:4*
against her will when what happens is already
her will: for it is no other than an instilled
eagerness to advance in holiness. She is animated with zeal for the task alotted her and
given livelier awareness of the fittingness of the
time. My bride, he says, it is time to act,* for   *Ps 118:126*
the winter is past* when no one could   *Sg 2:11*
work.* The rain too that covered the earth   *Jn 9:4*
with floods, that precluded tillage, that either
hindered the sowing of crops or destroyed
what was sown, that rain, I say, has quickly
vanished; 'it is over and gone, the flowers have
appeared in our land',* showing that the   *Sg 2:11*
warmth of spring is here, that it is seasonal to
work, that harvests and fruits are not far off.
Then he suggests both where and what she
should do first, saying: 'the time for pruning
has come.'* She is led out to the cultivation   *Sg 2:12*
of the vines. If they are to yield more abundant fruits to the farmers it is necessary that
sterile boughs be got rid of, that noxious ones
be cut away, that superfluous ones be pruned.
So much for the literal sense.

II. 3. Now let us see what is proposed spiri-
tually to our understanding by this kind of
historical narrative. I have told you that the
vines are souls or churches, and the reason
why this is so. You have heard it and have no
need to hear it again. That soul who is more
perfect is invited to watch over these, to correct them, to instruct them, to save them,
provided he is alotted this ministry not by his
own ambition but by the call of God, as
Aaron was.* What is this invitation but an   *Heb 5:4*

inward impulse of charity, lovingly inciting us
to zeal for our brother's salvation, to zeal for
the beauty of God's house,* for an increase in *Ps 25:8
his rewards, an increase in the fruits of his
righteousness,* the praise and glory of his *2 Cor 9:10
name?* The man who is charged with the *Phil 1:11
spiritual direction of others or with the duty
of preaching may believe with certainty—as
often as he feels himself inwardly moved by
genuine love of God—that the Bridegroom is
present, inviting him each time to the vineyards. To what end but that he may pluck up
and destroy, that he may build and plant?* *Jer 1:10

4.   However, since for this work, as for
everything under heaven, not every season is
good or suitable, he who invites also adds
that the time for pruning is come.* The *Sg 2:12
apostle knew it was present when he cried
out: 'See, now is the favorable time; now is
the day of salvation. We do nothing that
people might object to, so as not to bring dis-
credit on our function as God's servants.'* *2 Cor 6:2-3
Knowing that the time for pruning had
come,* he warned that everything faulty and *Sg 2:12
superfluous, everything that could give the
least offense and hinder the fruit of salvation, should be pruned and cut off. Hence he
said to a certain faithful cultivator of vines:
'Convince, rebuke and exhort',* indicating by *2 Tim 4:2
the first and second of these pruning and era-
dicating, in the last planting. This the Bridegroom said by the mouth of Paul about the
time for working.* But hear what he said to *Gal 6:10
his new bride by his own mouth about the
observance of seasons, though under other
images and words: 'Do you not say, "there are

yet four months, then comes the harvest"?
I tell you, lift up your eyes and see how the
fields are already white for harvest.'* Or   *Jn 4:35
again: 'The harvest is plentiful but the laborers are few; pray therefore the Lord of the
harvest to send out laborers into his harvest.'*   *Mt 9:37-38
And so, just as he showed in the first case that
now is the time to reap the harvest of souls, so
in the second case he declares that the time
has come to prune the spiritual vines, that is
souls or churches. Perhaps by using these
different words he wished to distinguish
between different realities, so that by the
harvest we understand the people, and by
vineyards the congregations of holy persons
living in community.

5. Now, the winter period, which he
intimates has passed, seems to me to refer
to that time when the Lord Jesus did not
walk openly among the Jews because they
plotted against him, wishing to kill him.*   *Jn 11:54
Hence he said to some of the disciples: 'My
time has not yet come, but your time is always here.'* And again: 'Go to the feast   *Jn 7:6
yourselves; I am not going.'* 'But he went up   *Jn 7:8
afterwards himself, not publicly but in private.'* The winter lasted therefore from then   *Jn 7:10
until the coming of the Holy Spirit, by whom
the numbed hearts of the faithful were
warmed as by fire, whom the Lord sent on
earth to this end.* Would you deny that it   *Acts 2:3;
was then winter when Peter sat at the char-   Lk 12:49
coal fire, with a heart no less cold than his
body? 'It was cold', the Gospel says. Great   *Jn 18:18
indeed was the cold that seized the heart of
the denier. But no wonder, since the fire had

been taken away from him. A short while before he was aflame with no small zeal because he was still close to the fire, this man who, for fear of losing it, drew his sword and cut off the servant's ear.* But it was not the time for pruning, and therefore he heard: 'Put your sword back in its place.'* That was the hour and power of darkness,* and any disciple who would then wield the sword, whether of steel or of the word, must either be cut down by the sword and gain no follower nor bear any fruit, or he himself would perish, driven to denial by the sword of fear, just as the word of the Lord immediately added: 'all who take the sword will perish by the sword'.* Which of the others would stand undismayed before the fearsome image of death when their leader himself, fore-armed by the bracing words of his Emperor so that being fore-warned he might strengthen the others,* trembled and gave way?

6. But neither he nor they were as yet clothed with power from on high;* and so it was not safe for them to go out into the vineyards, to use the tongue as a hoe and with the sword of the Spirit to prune the vines, to trim the branches to let them bear more fruit.* Even the Lord himself kept silent during his passion,* and did not when interrogated answer questions on many things;* He became, as the prophet said, 'like a man who does not hear, and in whose mouth are no rebukes.'* He did say: 'If I tell you, you will not believe me. But if I were to do the asking, you would not answer me.'* He knew the the time of pruning had not yet come, that

*Mt 26:51

*Mt 26:52
*Lk 22:53

*Mt 26:52

*Lk 22:32

*Lk 24:49

*Jn 15:2
*Mt 26:63
*Mt 27:12

*Ps 37:15

*Lk 22:67

the vine would not respond to the labors expended on it, that it would bear no fruit either of faith or good works. Why? Because it was winter in the hearts of the faithless,* because the wintry rains of malice still flooded the earth, more calculated to drown than to nourish the scattered seeds of the word,* and to frustrate any effort to cultivate the vines. *Jn 10:22

*Mt 13:22

7. What rains do you think I am now speaking of? Those which we see the rushing clouds pour upon the earth in a violent tempest? Not those. But those which men of a violent spirit cause to rise from earth to the heavens, whose 'slanders reach up to heaven while their tongues ply to and fro on earth'* like pestilential showers, making the earth itself a barren marsh, unfit for both plants and seeds. I do not mean those that we can see and touch, that are meant for the welfare of our bodies—about which God is no more concerned than he is about cattle.* Which then? Surely those which God's hand, not man's, has sown and planted, that germinate and take root in faith and love,* that bear the fruits of salvation if watered by good and timely rains. The souls for which Christ died.* Woe to the clouds that pour down bad rains; they make only mud, they do not produce fruit. *Ps 72:9

*1 Cor 9:9

*Eph 3:17

*Rom 14:15

III. Now just as there are good and bad trees, each bearing fruits that differ because of their differences—the good have good fruits, the bad bad*—so too, I think, are the clouds: The rains the good pour are good, the bad pour bad. Consider then if the Lord was *Mt 12:33

not intimating this difference in clouds and
rains to us when he said: 'I will command my
clouds that they rain no rain upon it'*—upon
the vineyard, of course. Why do you think he
so pointedly says 'my clouds', except that
there are bad clouds which are not his?
'Away with him, away with him', they said.
'Crucify him.'* O violent and stormy clouds!
O tempestuous rains! O torrent of wickedness,* fit rather to destroy than to fertilize!
Not less evil or bitter, though less violent in
its downpour, was that rain which followed
close behind: 'He saved others; he cannot save
himself. Let the Christ, the king of Israel,
come down now from the cross and we will
believe in him.'* The windy chatter of philo-
sophers was not good rain; it produced barrenness, not fertility. Much worse still were
those rains, the perverse dogmas of the heretics that brought forth thorns and thistles
instead of fruit.* The traditions of the Pharisees,* themselves bad clouds, were also a bad
rain that the Saviour condemned. And though
you may consider me unjust to Moses, for he
is a good cloud, I do not call everything
good which even he poured down, or else
I shall contradict him who said: 'I gave them',
that is the Jews, 'statutes that were not
good'—which certainly came through Moses—
'and ordinances by which they could not
have life.'* For example, that literal observance of the sabbath which enjoined but
gave no rest; the imposed rite of sacrifices;
the prohibition of eating pork and many
similar things condemned by Moses as unclean—this was a rain coming down entirely

*Is 5:6

*Jn 19:15

*Ps 17:5

*Mt 27:42

*Gen 3:18
*Mt 15:2

*Ezk 20:25

from that [Mosaic] cloud. I should hate it to
fall in any field or garden of mine. It may
have been good in its proper season, but if it
comes out of season I consider it no longer
good. Even a soft rain, a rain that falls gently,
is harmful if it is untimely.

8. As long as these pestilent waters flooded
and submerged the earth, then, the vineyards
did not come into season, nor could the bride
be invited to prune the vines. But when they
ebbed away the dry land appeared* and the **Wis 19:7*
flowers bloomed, showing that the time for
pruning was at hand. You ask when this was?
When do you think, if not when Christ's flesh
flowered again at the resurrection? This was
the first and greatest flower to appear in our
land, for Christ is the first fruit.* He, Jesus, is **1 Cor 15:20*
'the flower of the fields and the lily of the
valleys',* being the son, as was supposed, of **Sg 2:1*
Joseph of Nazareth,* which means a flower.[1] **Lk 3:23*
He appeared therefore the first flower but not
the only one. For many bodies of the saints
who had fallen asleep also arose,* and ap- **Mt 27:52*
peared in our land all brilliant like flowers.
They even 'entered the holy city where they
appeared to many'.* The people who were **Mt 27:53*
fruits of the saints. Their miracles were
flowers that, like flowers, produced the fruit
flowers that like flowers, produced the fruit
of faith. For when that rain of unbelief was
over and gone,* at least partially, there soon **Sg 2:11*
followed that 'free rain'* which the Lord had **Ps 67:10*

1. Bernard identifies Nazareth with the word "neṣer", as in Is 11,1.
Cf. Jerome, *Liber interpretationis hebraicorum nominum* (CCSL
72:62).

set aside for his inheritance, and the flowers began to appear. The Lord bestowed prosperity and our earth yielded its flowers,* so that on one day three thousand, on another five thousand people believed*—in a short time the number of flowers grew like this which means, the multitude of believers.* Nor could the front of malice overwhelm the flowers that appeared, nor destroy in advance, as it often does, the fruit of which they gave promise.

*Ps 84:13

*Acts 2:41; 4:4.

*Acts 5:14

9. For when all who had believed were clothed with power from on high,* men arose from their midst firm in the faith,* who despised the threats of men. They suffered indeed from a great many adversaries, but they did not cease from or abandon the performance and proclamation of the works of God.* In a spiritual way they fulfilled the words of the psalm: 'They sowed fields and planted vineyards and got a fruitful yield.'* In the course of time the storm was stilled, peace was restored to the earth, the vines grew and they were propagated and spread abroad and multiplied beyond counting.* Then at last the bride was invited to the vineyards, not to plant but to prune what had been planted. At the proper time too, for this task needed a period of peace. For how could it be possible when she was being persecuted? But also, to prune the vines is to grasp the two-edged swords, to wreak vengeance on the nations and chastisement on the peoples, to bind their kings with chains and their nobles with fetters of iron, to execute on them the prescribed judgment!* Even in a time of

*Lk 24:49
*1 Pet 5:9

*Ps 63:10

*Ps 106:37

*Ps 39:6

*Ps 149:6-9

peace all these things can scarcely be performed peacefully! Enough on this point.

IV. 10. This sermon could even had ended
here if I had first given each of you my customary warning about his vineyard. For who
has so completely cut away from himself all
superfluous things that he thinks he has
nothing worth pruning? Take my word for it,
what is pruned will sprout again, what is
banished will return, what is quenched will
blaze again, things lulled to sleep will re-
awaken. To prune once therefore is of little
worth. One must prune often, even, if possible, always, for you will always find something to prune if you aren't dishonest with
yourself. No matter what progress you make
in this life, you are wrong if you think vices
are dead when they are only suppressed.
Whether you like it or not, the Jebusite
dwells within your borders.* He can be sub-   *Judg 1:21*
dued but not exterminated. 'I know', said the
apostle, 'that nothing good dwells within
me.'* But this is not enough unless he also   *Rom 7:18*
admits that evil is within him. So he says:
'For I do not do the good I want to do, but
the evil I do not want is what I do. Now if I
do what I do not want, it is no longer I that
do it, but sin which dwells within me.'* If you   *Rom 7:19-20*
dare then, either prefer yourself to Paul—for
it is he who speaks—or admit with him that
you too are not lacking in vices. Virtue stands
in the midst of vices, and therefore needs not
only careful pruning but a trimming of the
ground about it. Otherwise one must fear that
as the vices steal upon it from all sides and

Mt 13:7

nibble at it, it will gradually wither, unbeknownst to you, and suffocate when overgrown.* In so great a hazard the only plan is to keep a sharp watch, and as soon as the buds appear to lop them off ruthlessly. Virtue and vices cannot prosper together: if the one is to flourish, the others must be checked. Remove the superfluous and the wholesome will thrive. Control cupidity and promote what is good. Let us apply ourselves to pruning. Let cupidity be pruned that virtue may grow strong.

11. For us, brothers, it is always time to prune, just as there is always a need. I am confident that for us the winter has now past. You know the winter I mean, that fear which is devoid of love, which, although it can lead everyone to wisdom perfects no one, because superabounding love drives it away as summer does the winter.* Summer means charity, which, if it has come, or rather because it has come—I am right in thinking you enjoy it—of necessity dries up every wintry rain, every anxious tear wrung from you by the bitter recollection of sin and fear of the judgment. Accordingly—and I say this without hesitation about many of you, if not all—this rain is now over and gone, for now the flowers appear as witnesses to a gentler rain. For summer too has its pleasant and enriching showers. What is sweeter than charity's tears? Charity weeps, but from love, not from sorrow; it weeps from desire, it weeps with those who weep.* I am convinced that a rain like this moistens your acts of obedience which I see so gladly. No murmuring taints them, no sadness overshadows them, but a certain

1 Jn 4:18

Rom 12:15

spiritual joy makes them delightful and radiant. They are like flowers that you always
carry in your hands.

12. Therefore if the winter is past, the
rain over and gone, if flowers have appeared
again in our land and the spring-like warmth
of spiritual grace indicates the time for pruning, what is left for us but to bend our energies totally to this work, so holy and so
necessary. Let us examine our ways and our
endeavors, as the prophet counsels,* and let   *Lam 3:40;
each one judge that he has progressed, not by   Jer 18:11
finding nothing to correct, but by correcting
what he does find. You will not have examined yourself in vain when you discover the
need for a new examination: your investigation never deceives you as often as you decide
that it needs repeating. But if you always do it
at the spur of need, you will do it always. Be
mindful therefore that you always have need
of heaven's help and of the mercy of the
Church's Bridegroom, Jesus Christ our Lord,
who is God over all, blessed for ever. Amen.*   *Rom 9:5

SERMON FIFTY-NINE

I. THE REASON WHY THE BRIDEGROOM
SAYS: 'IN OUR LAND'.   II. THE VOICE
OR MOURNING OF THE TURTLE-DOVE,
AND WHEN IT IS ESPECIALLY HEARD.
III. WHY ONLY ONE TURTLE-DOVE IS
SPOKEN OF, AND HER CHASTITY.   IV.
FAITH IS INCREASED BY WHAT THE
SOUND OF THE VOICE AND THE SIGHT
OF THE FLOWER SIGNIFY.

I. 1. 'THE VOICE OF THE TURTLE-DOVE is heard in our land.'* I can no longer hide the fact that for the second time he who is from heaven* speaks of the earth so agreeably and intimately, as if he were someone from the earth. He is the Bridegroom who, when announcing that the flowers had appeared in the land, added 'our [land]'. And how again he says: 'the voice of turtle-dove is heard in our land.'* Can this statement, so unusual, or even, if I may say it, so unworthy of God, lack significance? Nowhere, I think, will you find him speaking like this of heaven, nowhere else like this of earth. Notice then the utter happiness of hearing the God of heaven say: 'in our land'. 'Listen, all inhabitants of the earth, all peoples',* 'the Lord has done great things for us.'* He has

*Sg 2:12

*Jn 3:31

*Sg 2:12

*Ps 48:3
*Ps 125:3

120

done much for the earth, much for the bride,
whom he has been pleased to take to himself
from the earth. 'In our land', he says. This is
clearly not the language of domination but of
fellowship and intimate friendship. He speaks
as Bridegroom, not as lord. Think of it! He is
the Creator, and he makes himself one of us?
It is love that speaks, that knows no lordship.
This is a song of love, in fact, and meant to be
sustained only by lovers, not by others. God
loves too, though not through a gift distinct
from himself: he is himself the source of
loving. And therefore it is all the more
vehement, for he does not possess love, he is
love. And those whom he loves he calls
friends, not servants.* The master has become   *Jn 15:15
the friend; for he would not have called the
disciples friends if it were not true.

2. Do you see that even majesty yields
to love? That is how it is, brothers. Love
neither looks up to nor looks down on anybody. It regards as equal all who love each
other truly, bringing together in itself the
lofty and the lowly. It makes them not only
equal but one. Perhaps up till now you have
thought God should be an exception to this
law of love; but anyone who is united to the
Lord becomes one spirit with him.* Why   *1 Cor 6:17
wonder at this? He has become like one of
us.* But I said too little: not 'like one of us',   *Gen 3:22
but 'one of us'. It is not enough for him to be
on a par with men, he is a man. Hence he lays
claim to our land for himself, not as a possession but as his homeland. And why not
claim it? From there is his bride, from there
his bodily substance, from there the Bride-

*Eph 5:31

*Ps 113:24

groom himself, from there the two become one flesh.* If one flesh, why not also one homeland? 'The heavens are the Lord's heavens, but the earth he has given to the sons of men.'* Therefore as man he inherits the earth, as Lord he rules over it, as Creator he controls it, as Bridegroom he shares it. By saying 'in our land' he has disclaimed proprietorship over it, he has not disdained participation in it. These thoughts have been inspired by the great goodness of the Bridegroom's words, that he was pleased to say 'in our land'. Now let's look at the rest [of the text].

II. 3. 'The voice of the turtle-dove is heard in our land.' This is a sign that winter is past, but also a warning that the time for pruning is at hand. This is the literal sense. Usually the voice of the turtle-dove does not sound very sweet, but it suggests things that are sweet. If you buy the little bird she is cheap, but if you make her an object of discussion, her price is high. With her voice more akin to mourning than to singing, she reminds us that we are pilgrims. I listen willingly to the voice of the teacher who does not stir up applause for himself but compunction in me. You really resemble the turtle-dove if you preach repentance: and if you want your words to be convincing you must depend more on your repentance than on your eloquence. As in many situations but above all in this business, example is more effective than preaching. You will stamp your preaching with authority if you are conscious of accepting for yourself the values you preach. Actions speak louder

than words. Practice what you preach, and
not only will you correct me more easily
but also free yourself from no light reproach.
You will not be the target if someone says:
'They bind heavy burdens, hard to bear, and
lay them on men's shoulders; but they them-
selves will not move them with their finger.'*   *Mt 23:4*
Nor need you be afraid to hear: 'You who
teach others, will you not teach yourself?'*   *Rom 2:21*

4. 'The voice of the turtle-dove is heard
in our land.' As long as men's reward for wor-
shipping God was only of the earth, even the
earth that flows with milk and honey,* they   *Deut 6:3*
failed to see themselves as pilgrims on earth,*   *Heb 11:13*
nor did they mourn like the turtle-dove as if
recalling their homeland. Instead they con-
fused exile with homeland, pampering themselves with rich foods and drinking honeyed
wine.* So for a long time the voice of the   *Neh 8:10*
turtle-dove was not heard in our land. When
the promise of the kingdom became known,
then men realized that they had no lasting
city here,* and they began to seek with all   *Heb 13:14*
their longing the one that is to come. It was
then that the voice of the turtle-dove was first
heard clearly in our land. Now meanwhile a
holy soul ardently desires the presence of
Christ, he endures the deferment of the kingdom painfully, he salutes from afar with
groans and sighs the homeland he longs for—
do you not think that anybody on this earth
who behaves like this is in the position of the
chaste and mournful turtle-dove? From then
'the voice of the turtle-dove is heard in our
land'. Why should the absence of Christ not
move me to frequent tears and daily groan-

ings? 'Lord, all that I long for is known to you, my sighing is no secret from you.'* 'I am worn out with groaning' as you know; but happy is the man who can say: 'Every night I drench my pillow and soak my bed with tears.'* These groanings are to be found not only in me but in 'all those who have longed for his appearing'.* This is what he himself said: 'Can the wedding guests mourn as long as the bridegroom is with them? But the days will come when the bridegroom will be taken away from them, and then they will mourn',* as if he were to say: then the voice of the turtle-dove will be heard.

5. So it is, good Jesus: those days came. For 'creation itself has been groaning in one great act of giving birth',* 'longing for the revealing of the sons of God'.* 'And not only creation, but we too groan inwardly as we wait for adoption as sons, for our bodies to be set free',* for we know that to live in the body means to pilgrimage apart from you.* Nor are these groanings in vain, for heaven's answer is merciful: 'Because the poor are despoiled, because the needy groan, I will now arise', says the Lord.'* That mourning voice was heard too in the days of the Fathers, but it was rare, and each person's groaning was within himself. Hence one of them said: 'My secret to myself, my secret to myself'.* But he who said, 'My groaning is not hidden from you',* clearly showed that it was hidden, because it was hidden from all but God. Therefore in those days one could not say 'the voice of the turtle-dove is heard in our land', because it was the secret of a few and

*Ps 37:10

*Ps 6:7

*2 Tim 4:8

*Mt 9:15

*Rom 8:22
*Rom 8:19

*Rom 8:23
*2 Cor 5:6

*Ps 11:6

*Is 24:16

*Ps 37:10

not yet divulged to the multitude. But when the public proclamation was made: 'Seek the things that are above, where Christ is, seated at the right hand of God',* that dove-like mourning became of relevance to all, and the reason for mourning was the same for all, because all had knowledge of the Lord, as we read in the prophet: ' "They shall all know me, from the least of them to the greatest", says the Lord.'*

*Col 3:1

*Jer 31:34

III. 6. But if the mourners be many, what does he mean by speaking of one? The voice of the turtle-dove, he says. Why not turtle-doves? Perhaps the Apostle explains it where he says that 'the Spirit himself intercedes for us with sighs too deep for words'.* That's how it is: he who inspires men to mourn is introduced as mourning. And however great the number whose mourning you hear, it is his voice that sounds through the lips of all. But why not his, since he forms every voice in the mouth [crying] for the needs of each? Indeed 'to each one is given the manifestation of the Spirit for the common good'.* A person's voice makes him manifest, and indicates his presence. Listen then to how the Holy Spirit has a voice, according to Scripture: 'The Spirit breathes where he wills, and you hear his voice, but you do not know whence he comes or whither he goes.'* Although that dead teacher who taught the dead the letter that brings death* was ignorant of this, we know, we who 'have passed out of death and into life* through the life-giving Spirit.* By the light that he gives us, by a sure experience

*Rom 8:26

*1 Cor 12:7

*Jn 3:8

*2 Cor 3:6

*1 Jn 3:14
*1 Cor 15:45

day after day, we are convinced that our
desires and groanings come from him and go
to God, to find mercy there in the eyes of
God. For when did God make the voice of his
own Spirit ineffectual? He 'knows what is the
mind of the Spirit, because the Spirit intercedes for the saints according to the will
of God'.*

*Rom 8:27

7.   The turtle-dove is commended not only
for its mourning but also for its chastity. For
it was by merit of this that it was worthy
to be offered up as a sacrificial victim for the
virgin birth. Scripture says 'a pair of turtle-
doves or two young doves'.* And though
elsewhere the Holy Spirit is usually designated by the dove, yet because it is a lustful
bird, it is not a fit offering for the Lord
except when it was young and ignorant of
lust. But no age is stated for the turtle-dove,
for its chastity is acknowledged at any age. It
is content with one mate; if he is lost it does
not take another, thus arguing against man's
tendency to marry more than once. Now,
although as a remedy for incontinence this is
only a venial fault, still the incontinence that
demands it is a disgrace. It is shameful that
reason cannot lead man to that uprightness
which nature achieves in the bird. During its
widowhood you may see the turtle-dove
fulfilling with unflagging zeal the duties of
holy widowhood. Everywhere you see it
alone, everywhere you hear it mourning;
you never see it perched on a green bough—a
lesson to you to avoid the green but poisonous shoots of sensual pleasure. Rather it
haunts the mountain ridges and the tops of

*Lk 2:24

trees, to teach us to shun the pleasures of earth and to love those of heaven.*

8. One may conclude from this that the preaching of chastity is also the voice of the turtle-dove. From the very beginning this voice was not heard on the earth, but instead that other: 'Be fruitful and multiply and fill the earth'.* This call to chastity would have been to no purpose when the homeland of those risen had not yet been opened up, where men in a far happier state 'neither marry nor are given in marriage',* but are like the angels in heaven. Do you think the time was then suitable for that voice, when every barren Israelite lay under a curse, when the Patriarchs themselves practiced polygamy, when a brother was compelled by law to beget children for a brother who had died childless?* But when the mouth of the heavenly turtle-dove intoned its praises for those eunuchs who have gelded themselves for the sake of the kingdom of heaven,* and when that counsel on virginity from another chaste turtle-dove everywhere prevailed,* then for the first time it could be truly said that 'the voice of the turtle-dove is heard in our land'.

IV. 9. So then, the flowers have appeared in our land and the voice of the turtle-dove is heard: the truth is ascertained both by the eye and the ear. The voice is heard, the flower is seen. According to our previous interpretation* the flowers stand for miracles which, joined to the voice, bring forth the fruit of faith. Although faith comes from hearing* it is strengthened by seeing. The voice resounded,

Postcommunion, Advent II (old Missal)

Gen 9:1

Lk 20:35-36

Mt 22:24

Mt 19:12

1 Cor 7:25

Sermon 51:2

Rom 10:17

the flower blossomed, and truth sprang up
from the earth by the worship of the faithful,* word and sign equally concurring in
witness to the faith. These testimonies have
become easy to believe as the flower corrob-
orates the witness of the word, the eye that
of the ear. What is heard confirms what is
seen, so that the witness of two*—the ear and
the eye—is validated. That is why the Lord
said: 'Go and tell John'—he was speaking to his
disciples—'what you have seen and heard.'* He
could not have expressed to them more
briefly or more clearly the certainty of the
faith. In a short time that same belief was
spread over the whole world, and by the same
condensed reasoning. 'What you have seen and
heard',* he said. O word abridged, yet living
and powerful!* I proclaim without misgiving
what I have grasped by ear and eyes. The
trumpet of salvation sounds, miracles gleam,
and the world believes. It is quickly convinced of what is said, borne out by signs of
power. You read that the apostles 'went forth
and preached everywhere, while the Lord
worked with them and confirmed the message
by the signs that attended it'.* You read that
he was transfigured on the mountain with
staggering brightness and yet that the voice
from on high bore witness to him.* Likewise
at the Jordan, you read of the dove identify-
ing him and the voice giving testimony.* So
these two, voice and sign, everywhere equally
co-operate, by divine generosity, to inspire
the faith, for by both these windows a wide
entrance to the mind lies open for the truth.

10. [The text] continues: 'The fig tree

*Ps 84:12

*Mt 18:16

*Lk 7:22

*Mt 11:4
*Heb 4:12

*Mk 16:20

*Mt 17:5

*Mt 3:17

has put forth its green figs.'* Let us not
eat them; they are unfit for eating because
they are unripe. They resemble good figs in
appearance, but not in flavor, and perhaps
signify hypocrisy. We should not throw them
away however, perhaps we shall need them at
another time. In any case they will fall prematurely of their own accord, 'like the grass
on the housetops, which withers before it is
plucked up'.* I take this to be a reference to
hypocrites. They are not mentioned in this
wedding song without reason. Even if not fit
to eat they can serve another purpose. Many
things besides eatables must be provided for a
wedding feast. This is a matter I think must
not be passed over, but whatever its significance I do not want to confine its discussion
to a short space at the end of this sermon. I
defer it to another day and a freer time. It
will be up to you then to decide whether it has
been necessary; may your prayers gain for me
the opportunity and the competence to express what I feel, for your spiritual well-being,
for the praise and glory of the Church's
Bridegroom, our Lord Jesus Christ, 'who is
God over all, blessed for ever. Amen'.*

*Sg 2:13

*Ps 128:6

*Rom 9:5

SERMON SIXTY

I. THE FIG TREE AND ITS GREEN FIGS:
WHAT THEY ARE AND WHEN IT PRO-
DUCES THEM. II. THE VINE, THE
FLOWER, GREEN FIGS AND VINES
SEEN FIGURATIVELY.

*Sg 2:13

*Sg 2:12

I. 1. 'THE FIG TREE has put forth its green figs.'* We begin now where we left off. He had said that the time for pruning had come,* both because the flowers had appeared and because the turtle dove's voice was heard. He affirms it yet again now by the forming of green figs, for the signs of the seasons are observed not only in the flowers and the turtle dove's voice, but also in the fig tree. The air is never milder than when the fig tree puts forth its green figs. The fig has no flowers, but when other trees flower it puts forth fig buds. And just as flowers bloom and fade, good for nothing but to herald the fruits that follow, so the green figs bud only to fall prematurely, no good themselves to eat, and make room for those that will ripen. Thus therefore, as I said, the Bridegroom takes the signs of the season as an argument to urge the bride not to loiter on the way to the vineyards, lest the task which comes in its proper time be lost. So much for the literal sense.

2. But what of the spiritual sense? Clearly, we are here considering not a fig tree but people: God's concern is for men, not for trees.* The fig tree represents people, frail in flesh, limited in intelligence, shallow of mind, whose first fruits—to continue the comparison—are green and earthy. For the popular trend is not to seek first the kingdom of God and his righteousness,* but, as the apostle says, to be concerned about worldly affairs, about pleasing their wives or the wives their husbands.* Those [who marry] will indeed have trials of the flesh;* but we do not deny that on the last day they will attain to the fruits of faith if they shall have made a last good confession,* and especially if they compensate by almsgiving for their worldliness.* Therefore the first fruits of the people deserve the name fruit no more than do the fig buds of the fig trees. If afterwards they bear fruits that befit repentance*—for it is not the spiritual which is first but the physical*—it will be said to them: 'what return did you get from the things of which you are now ashamed?'*

3. I do not think myself free to apply this passage to people in general, however: one person is distinctly referred to. For he did not speak of many trees and say 'they put forth', but of one: 'the fig tree has put forth its green figs',* meaning, I think, the Jewish people. How often the Saviour uses this image in the Gospel! For example: 'A man had a fig tree planted in his vineyard',* etc. Also: 'Look at the fig tree and all the trees'.*

*1 Cor 9:9

*Mt 6:33

*1 Cor 7:38
*1 Cor 7:28

*1 Tim 6:12

*Gal 5:19;
Dan 4:27

*Lk 3:8

*1 Cor 15:46

*Rom 5:21

*Sg 2:13

*Lk 13:6
*Lk 21:29

And Nathanael was told: 'When you were
under the fig tree I saw you.'* Another time
he cursed the fig tree because he found no
fruit on it.* The fig tree is a good image, for
though sprouting from the sound patriarchal
root it never aimed to reach toward the sky,
never aimed at lifting itself from the ground,
never responded to the root by putting out
branches, by blooming into flower, by an
abundance of fruit. O stunted, twisted, knotty
tree, how completely ill-suited to you is your
root. For the root is holy.* Does anything
worthy of it appear in your branches? 'The
fig tree has put forth its green figs!' Worthless
seed, you have not brought these forth from
that noble root. What it contains is of the
Holy Spirit,* and so in every respect refined
and sweet. Where then do these green figs
come from? And really what does that nation
have that is not crude? Neither their actions
nor their inclinations nor their understanding;
not even the rites with which they worship
God. Their actions are summed up in strife,
their whole orientation was to wealth, their
understanding was darkened in literalism,
they worshipped with the blood of sheep
and cattle.

4. But someone says: Since that nation
never stopped producing these green figs,
then the time for pruning was always present,
because the two events are contemporaneous.
That is not the case. We say that women have
begotten children not when they are in labor
but when they have given birth. And we say
that trees have flowered, not when they begin
to flower but when they are full-blown.

*Jn 1:48

*Mk 11:13-14

*Rom 11:16

*Mt 1:20

Similarly it is said here that the fig tree has put forth its green figs when it has produced not a few but the whole lot, that is, when the production is completed. Do you ask when this climax took place for that people? Their malice was complete when they killed Christ, in accord with his own prediction to them: 'Fill up the measure of your fathers.'*   *Mt 23:32 So when he was about to yield up his spirit on the gibbet he said: 'It is accomplished.'*   *Jn 19:30 What an accomplishment this accursed fig tree brought to its green figs, condemned as it was to an endless sterility! How much worse were these last fruits than those before!*   *Mt 12:45 Worthless in the beginning, they ended up pernicious and poisonous. What a crude and snakey disposition, to hate the man who both heals men's bodies and saves their souls! No less crude and obviously cow-like their understanding, that did not recognize God even in God's works!*   *Ps 27:5

5. Perhaps a Jew will complain that I have gone to excess in insulting him by calling his understanding cow-like. But let him read Isaiah and he will hear something even less flattering: 'The ox knows its owner, and the ass its master's crib; but Israel does not know me, my people does not understand.'*   *Is 1:3 See, Jew, I am kinder to you than your own prophet. I have put you on a level with beasts, he sets you below them. Yet the prophet did not speak here in his own person but in that of God, who proclaims by his very works that he is God: 'Even though you do not believe me', he said, 'believe the works';*   *Jn 10:38 'and if I am not doing the works of my

*Jn 10:37

Father, then do not believe me.'* Even this
did not wake them up to understanding.
Neither the expulsion of devils nor the obedience of the elements nor the raising of the
dead could banish from them this bestial and
more than bestial stupidity. Out of this
blindness no less monstrous than miserable
they rushed into that horrifying and incredi-
bly crude crime of laying sacrilegious hands
on the majestic Lord. From that moment it
could be said that the fig tree had put forth its
green figs, for the institutions of the Jewish
law were drawing to a close, so that, in
accord with the old prophecy, as the new was

*Lev 26:10

coming on the old would be cleared away.*
Surely these are not unalike: the green figs
fall and give place to the good figs that sprout
after them. To the bride he said: as long as
the fig tree continued to produce its green
figs I did not call you, knowing it could not
at the same time produce the best figs. Now
that those which had to come first are already produced it is no longer untimely for
me to invite you, for the good and wholesome fruits are known to come on as the bad
ones are discarded.

II. 6. And now he says: 'The vines in flower

*Sg 2:13

yield their sweet perfume',* which is a good
sign that the fruit is forming. This perfume
drives away snakes. They say that when vines
are flowering every poisonous reptile leaves
the place, being unable to endure the perfume
of fresh flowers. I want our novices to take
note of this, and to act with confidence,
reflecting on the spirit they have received,

whose first fruits the devils cannot tolerate. If initial fervor can achieve this what will finished perfection do? The fruit depends on the flower, and the quality of the taste is judged from how strong the thing smells. 'The vines in flower yield their sweet perfume.' This is how it was in the beginning: new life ensued from the preaching, new grace for those who believed;* they lived virtuously among the pagans† and bore the good perfume of Christ* wherever they went. Good perfume means good witness. It comes from right behavior as perfume comes from the flower. And since in the early days of the infant church faithful souls, like so many spiritual vines, seemed laden with this kind of flower and perfume, being well thought of even by outsiders,* I think it not unfitting to apply this phrase to them. To what end? That those who had not believed might find in it a challenge, and reflecting on the believers' upright conduct, would themselves glorify God,* and thus for them the perfume of life would lead to life.* Not undeservedly then are they said to have given off a perfume if they have sought in their own good reputation not glory for themselves but other men's salvation. Otherwise, as some did, they could have made godliness a means of gain,* for instance by ostentation or avarice. This however would be not to give but to sell the perfume. But because everything they did was done in love,* they surely did not sell the perfume, but gave it as a gift.

*Rom 6:4
†1 Pet 2:12
*2 Cor 2:15

*1 Tim 3:7

*1 Pet 2:12

*2 Cor 2:16

*1 Tim 6:5

*1 Cor 16:14

7. If the vines mean souls, the flower work, the perfume good reputation, then what

does the fruit mean? Martyrdom. Surely the fruit of the vine is the martyr's blood. [The psalmist] says: 'When he shall give sleep to his beloved: behold the inheritance of the Lord are children; the reward, the fruit of the womb.'* I almost said 'the fruit of the vine'. Why should I not speak of the blood of the innocent, the blood of the righteous, as the purest blood of the grape?* Is it not new red must, tested and precious,* from the vineyard of Sorek,† trodden out in the wine-press of suffering? For 'precious in the sight of the Lord is the death of his saints'.* This is how I interpret the words: 'The vines in flower yield their sweet perfume.'

8. If we choose to apply this text to the seasons of grace, this is how. But if we prefer to refer it to the Fathers—for 'the vineyard of the Lord of hosts is the house of Israel'*—the meaning will be: the prophets and patriarchs inhaled the perfume of Christ, who was to be born and to die as man, but they did not then give off that same perfume because they did not reveal in the flesh him whom they perceived in advance in their minds. They did not give off their perfume or publish their secret, but awaited its revelation in due time. Who then could understand the wisdom hidden in a mystery* and not as yet shown forth in bodily form? So indeed the vines did not then give off their perfume. But they gave it off later, when after many generations they gave to the world the Christ sprung from them in the flesh by a virginal birth.* Then indeed these spiritual vines gave off their perfume 'when the kindness and the human-

Ps 126:2-3

Deut 32:14
Is 28:16
†Cf. Is 5:2, Judg 16:14: Heb. soreq = *choice red wine.*
Ps 115:15

Is 5:7

1 Cor 2:7

Rom 9:5

ness of God our Saviour appeared',* and the
world began to enjoy the presence of one
whom in his absence few had anticipated.
There was, for example, the man who in
touching Jacob, perceived Christ. He said:
'See, the smell of my son is as the smell of a
field which the Lord has blessed';* as he said
this however he kept his happiness to himself, he did not share it with any one. 'But
when the fullness of time had come, God sent
forth his Son, born of woman, born under the
law, to redeem those who were under the
law.'* Then straightway the perfume that
was in him diffused itself everywhere, so that
the Church, perceiving it even from the ends
of the earth,* exclaimed: 'Your name is oil
poured out',* and the maidens hastened to the
oil's perfume. Thus that vine gave off its perfume, and others too in whom this perfume of
life* existed gave it forth at that time. Why
wouldn't they? From them Christ came as
man.* The vines therefore were said to give
off a perfume either because those who were
faithful strewed a good opinion of themselves
everywhere or because the prophecies and
revelations of the Fathers were made known
to the world and their perfume penetrated to
every land,* just as the apostle said: 'Great
indeed is the mystery of our religion: he was
manifested in the flesh, vindicated in the
spirit, seen by angels, preached among the
nations, believed in in the world, taken up
in glory.'*

*Tit 3:4

*Gen 27:27

*Gal 4:4-5

*Ps 60:3
*Sg 1:2-3

*2 Cor 2:16

*Rom 9:5

*Ps 18:5

*1 Tim 3:16

III. 9. It would be strange indeed if neither
the fig tree nor the vines had anything to im-

Rom 12:3

Rom 12:11

Phil 2:15

1 Jn 4:18

1 Cor 13:8

*Cf. William of
St Thierry,
Spec fid 1:1;
CF 15:3–4.
†Rom 8:24
**1 Cor 13:8

Lk 10:27

prove our lives. I think that this passage has a moral sense. I say then that by the grace of God which is in us* we have both fig trees and vines in our midst. The fig trees are the gentle in character, the vines those aglow with the Spirit.* Everyone who lives among us in harmony with the community, who not only mingles with his brothers without complaining, but with a very friendly attitude even makes himself available to all for any occasion of loving service,* why should I not very fittingly speak of him as a fig tree? If he first sprouts his green figs it is necessary that he shed them, for instance the fear of judgment that is driven out by perfect love,* and the bitterness of sinning which is sure to yield to sincere confession, the infusion of grace and an abundant outpouring of tears. There are other similar things too that like green figs precede sweet fruit, things you can reflect on by yourselves.

10. Let me add just one further remark in connection with this: consider whether even the gifts of knowledge, prophecy, tongues and the like, may be counted among the green figs. Like green figs they must fall away and give place to better things, as the apostle said: knowledge will vanish, prophecies will be swept away, tongues will cease.* Understanding will exclude even faith, and vision must follow upon hope.* 'For who hopes for what he sees?'† Only love never fails,** but only that love by which God is loved with all one's heart, all one's mind and all one's strength.* Hence I would on no account reckon it among the green figs, nor would

I say it pertains to the fig tree at all, but to the vines. Now those who are vines reveal themselves to us as more austere than amiable, they take action in an eager frame of mind, they are zealous for discipline, rigorous in correcting abuses, and thus aptly make their own the psalmist's words: 'Do I not hate those who hate you, O Lord, and loathe those who defy you?'* and, 'zeal for your house devours me'.* The one seems to me to excel in love of neighbor, the other in love of God, But let us pause here under this vine and this fig tree* in the shade of God's love and our neighbor's. Both loves are mine when I love you, Lord Jesus, my neighbor because you are a man and showed mercy to me,* and nevertheless you are God over all, blessed for ever. Amen.*

*Ps 138:21
*Ps 68:10

*1 Kgs 4:25

*Lk 10:36-37
*Rom 9:5

SERMON SIXTY-ONE

I. THOUGHTS ON THE EXPRESSION: 'MY DOVE IN THE CLEFTS OF THE ROCK', AND WHAT THE CLEFTS OF THE ROCK MEAN. II. THAT THE WISE MAN'S HOME IS IN THIS ROCK, WHICH IS A VERY SAFE DWELLING. III. THE WOUNDS OF CHRIST REPRESENT THE BACK OF GOD, THEY ARE THE CLEFTS OF THE ROCK AND IN THEM THE DOVE LIVES.

I. 1. 'ARISE MY LOVE, MY BRIDE, and come.'* The bridegroom draws attention to the greatness of his love by repeating words of love. Now repetition is the sign of affection, and since he again invites his beloved to work on the vines, he shows his concern for the salvation of souls. Now you have heard that the vines mean souls. But let us not pause to no purpose on what has been explained. Look at what follows. Never yet, as far as I recall, has he mentioned the bride openly in this whole work, except when she goes to the vineyards and draws near the wine of love. When she will have attained to it and become perfect she will celebrate a spiritual marriage; and they shall be two, not in one flesh but in one spirit,* as the apostle says: 'He who is united

Sg 2:13

Eph 5:31

140

to the Lord becomes one spirit with him.'*   **1 Cor 6:17*

2. [The bridegroom] continues: 'My dove in the clefts of the rock, in the crannies of the wall, show me your face, let your voice sound in my ears.'* He loves and goes on speaking   **Sg 2:14* the language of love. A second time he affectionately calls her dove, his dove, and claims her as his own; and what she was wont to ask so earnestly of him he now in his turn requests of her—to see her and to hear her voice. He acts like a bridegroom, but as one who is shy, who shrinks from public view and wants to enjoy his pleasures in an out of the way spot, 'in the clefts of the rock and the crannies of the wall'.* Imagine the bride-   **Ibid.* groom therefore saying: 'Don't be afraid, my love, that this work in the vineyard to which we are urging you will prevent or interrupt the business of love. It will surely provide opportunities for that, which we both equally desire. The vineyards have walls, of course, and these are welcome shelters for the shy.' This is a word play. Why shouldn't I call it play? For where is the seriousness in all these words? The external sound is not worth hearing unless the Spirit within helps our weak understanding.* Therefore let us not dally   **Rom 8:26* outside, lest we seem pre-occupied with the allurements of lust, but listen with modest ears to the sermon on love that is at hand. And when you consider the lovers themselves, think not of a man and a woman but of the Word and the soul. And if I should say Christ and the Church the same applies, except that the word Church signifies not one soul but the unity or rather unanimity of

many. Nor must you think of the 'clefts of the rock' and 'the crannies of the wall' as hiding-places for wicked carryings-on, or else some suspicion from the powers of darkness will straightway take hold of you.

3. Another writer glosses this passage differently, seeing in the clefts of the rock the wounds of Christ.* And quite correctly, for Christ is the rock.† Good the clefts that strengthen our faith in the resurrection and the divinity of Christ. [The apostle] exclaimed: 'My Lord and my God'.** What was the source of these inspired words if not the clefts of the rock? Within them 'the sparrow finds a home, and the swallow a nest where she may lay her young';* in them the dove finds safety and fearlessly watches the circling hawk. This is why he says: 'My dove is the clefts of the rock.'* The dove's reply: 'He has set me high upon a rock';* and again: 'He set my feet upon a rock.'*

II. The wise man builds his house upon a rock, because there he will fear the violence neither of storms nor of floods.* Is on the rock not good? Set high on the rock,* secure on the rock, I stand on the rock firmly. I am secure from the enemy, buttressed against a fall, all because I am raised up from the earth.* For everything earthly is uncertain and perishable. Our homeland is in heaven,* and we are not afraid of falling or being thrown down. The rock, with its durability and security, is in heaven. 'The rock is a refuge for the hedgehog.'* And really where is there safe sure rest for the weak except

*Gregory the Great, In Cantica, II,15; PL 79: 499D; & Aponius: Explanatio in Cantica, IV (ed H Bottino-I. Martini [Rome 1843] p 82). †1 Cor 10:4

**Jn 20:28

*Ps 83:4

*Sg 2:14
*Ps 26:6
*Ps 39:3

*Mt 7:24
*Ps 26:6

*Jn 12:32
*Phil 3:20

*Ps 103:18

in the Saviour's wounds? There the security of
my dwelling depends on the greatness of his
saving power. The world rages, the body
oppresses, the devil lays his snares: I do not
fall because I am founded on a rock.* *Lk 6:48*
sinned gravely, my conscience is disturbed
but not confounded, because I shall remember
the wounds of the Lord. For 'he was wounded
for our transgressions'.* What sin is so deadly *Is 53:5*
as not to be forgiven in the death of Christ?
If therefore a medicine so powerful and efficacious finds entrance to my mind, no disease, however virulent, can frighten me.

4. It is clear then that [Cain] erred when
he said: 'My wickedness is too great for me
to hope for pardon,'* unless he was not one *Gen 4:13*
of Christ's members, and had no share in the
merits of Christ, so as to assume as his own,
to claim as his own, what was his own, as
a member shares what belongs to the head.
But as for me, whatever is lacking in my own
resources I appropriate for myself from the
heart of the Lord, which overflows with
mercy. And there is no lack of clefts by
which they are poured out. They pierced his
hands and his feet,* they gored his side with *Ps 21:17*
a lance,* and through these fissures I can *Jn 19:34*
suck honey from the rock and oil from the
flinty stone*—I can taste and see that the *Deut 32:13*
Lord is good.* He was thinking thoughts of *Ps 33:9*
peace* and I did not know it.† 'For who has *Jer 29:11*
known the mind of the Lord, or who has been †Gen 28:16
his counsellor?'* But the nail that pierced *Rom 11:34*
him has become for me a key unlocking the
sight of the Lord's will. Why should I not
gaze through the cleft? The nail cries out, the

wound cries out that God is truly in Christ, reconciling the world to himself.* 'The iron pierced his soul'* and his heart has drawn near,* so that he is no longer one who cannot sympathize with my weaknesses.* The secret of his heart is laid open through the clefts of his body; that mighty mystery of loving is laid open,* laid open too the tender mercies of our God, in which the morning sun from on high has risen upon us.* Surely his heart* is laid open through his wounds! Where more clearly than in your wounds does the evidence shine that you, Lord, 'are good and forgiving, abounding in steadfast love'?* No one shows greater mercy than he who lays down his life for those who are judged and condemned.*

5. My merit therefore is the mercy of the Lord. Surely I am not devoid of merit as long as he is not of mercy. And if the Lord abounds in mercy,* I too must abound in merits. But what if I am aware of my many failings? Then, where failings abounded, grace abounded all the more.* And if the mercies of the Lord are from eternity to eternity,* I for my part will chant the mercies of the Lord forever.* But would this be my own righteousness? 'Lord, I will be mindful of your righteousness only.'* For that is also mine, since God has made you my righteousness.* Ought I to be afraid that the one will not be enough for us both? No, this is not the short cloak to which the prophet referred, that cannot cover two.* 'Your righteousness is an everlasting righteousness.'* What is longer than eternity? A righteousness that is ample and everlasting will

*2 Cor 5:19
*Ps 104:18
*Ps 54:22
*Heb 4:15

*1 Tim 3:16

*Lk 1:78
heart = viscera
  (passim)

*Ps 85:5

*Jn 15:13

*2 Sam 24:14

*Rom 5:20
*Ps 102:17
*Ps 88:1

*Ps 70:16

*1 Cor 1:30

*Is 28:20

*Ps 118:142

amply cover both you and me. In me indeed it covers a multitude of sins,* but in you, Lord, a treasury of loving-kindness, a wealth of goodness.* These are stored up for me in the clefts of the rock. How vast in them the store of your abounding goodness,* hidden certainly, but only from those who perish!* Why should what is holy be given to dogs, or pearls to pigs?* To us however God has revealed them by his Spirit,* and has even led us by the open clefts into the holy place.* What an abundance of goodness is here, what fulness of grace, what perfection of virtue!

    6. I will go then to these storerooms so richly endowed; taking the prophet's advice I shall leave the cities and dwell in the rock.* I shall be as the dove nesting in the highest point of the cleft, so that like Moses in his cleft of the rock I may be able to see at least the back of the Lord as he passes by.* For who can look on his face as he stands, on the glory of the unchangeable God, but he who is introduced not only to the holy place but to the holy of holies.

III. This contemplation of his back is no small favor, not to be despised. Let Herod despise him; but the more despicable he shows himself to Herod, the less I shall despise him. For this view of the Lord's back holds something that delights. Who knows whether God will turn and forgive,* and leave a blessing behind him? There will be a time when he will show his face and we shall be saved.* But meantime may he meet us with choicest blessings,† with those he is

*Jas 5:20

*Rom 2:4

*Ps 30:20
*2 Cor 2:15

*Mt 7:6
*1 Cor 2:10
*Heb 9:12

*Jer 48:28

*Ex 33:22-23

*Joel 2:14

*Ps 79:4
†Ps 20:4

accustomed to leave behind himself. One day
he will show his face in its dignity and glory,
now let him show 'the back' of his gracious
concern. He is great in his kingdom, but so
gentle on the cross. In this vision may he
come to meet me, in the other may he fill
me full. 'In your presence', says the psalmist,
'you shall fill me with joy'.* Each is a saving
vision, each is amiable; but the one in greatness, the other in lowliness: the one in splendor, the other in pale shadow.

7. [The psalmist] says next: the back of
his back is like pale gold.* Why should he not
grow pale in death? Better pale gold than
glittering brass; 'the foolishness of God is
wiser than men.'* Gold is the Word, gold is
wisdom. This gold discolored itself, conceal-
ing the form of God and displaying the form
of a servant. It also discolored the Church,
which says: 'Do not gaze at me because I am
swarthy, because the sun has scorched me.'*
So then, her back is like pale gold, because
she did blush at the swarthiness of the cross,
she was not terrified by the bitterness of the
passion, she did not flee from the ugliness of
the wounds. She even takes joy in them,* and
hopes that her last end may bear their likeness.* Accordingly she hears [the words]:
'My dove in the clefts of the rock',* because
all her affections are preoccupied with the
wounds of Christ; she abides in them by constant meditation. From this comes endurance
for martyrdom, for this her immense trust
in the Most High. The martyr need not be
afraid of raising his bloodless and bruised face
to him by whose wounds he is healed,* to

*Ps 15:11

*Ps 67:14

*1 Cor 1:25

*Sg 1:5

*Is 42:1

*Num 23:10
*Sg 2:14

*Is 53:5

present to him a glorious likeness of his death, even in the paleness of gold. Why should he fear, since the Lord himself says to him: 'show me your face'?* And why? It seems to *Sg 2:14* me he wishes to reveal himself; he wants to be seen rather than to see. What is there that he does not see? He by whom nothing is unseen, not even if someone hides himself—he does not require a person to show himself.* He *Jn 2:25* wants to be seen, then. The kindly captain wants the faithful soldier to lift up face and eyes to His own wounds, so as to strengthen his purpose, and by his own example to give him greater courage to endure.

8. While gazing on the Lord's wounds he will indeed not feel his own. The martyr remains jubilant and triumphant though his whole body is mangled; even while the steel is gashing his sides he looks around with courage and elation at the holy blood pouring from his flesh. Where then is the soul of the martyr? In a safe place, of course; in the rock, of course; in the heart of Jesus, of course, in wounds open for it to enter. Left to its own strength it would surely have felt the penetrating steel; it would not endure the pain; it would be overpowered and reject the faith. But now that it dwells in the rock* is it *Jer 48:28* any wonder if it endures as rock does? Nor should we wonder if, exiled from the body, it does not feel bodily pains. Insensibility does not bring this about, love does. For the feelings are not lost, they are leashed. And pain is not absent, it is scorned. From the rock therefore comes the courage of the martyr, from it obviously his power to drink the

*Mt 20:22

*Ps 22:5

*2 Esdr 8:10

*Sg 2:14

*Mt 10:32

*Rom 9:5

Lord's cup.* And this intoxicating cup—how wonderful it is!* Wonderful, I say, and sweet, no less to the commander looking on than to the conquering soldier. 'For the joy of the Lord is our strength.'* Why shouldn't he be joyful to hear so brave a testimony? He even longs for it with eagerness, and says: 'Let me hear your voice.'* Nor will he be slow to repay the favor, in accord with his promise: no sooner does a man acknowledge him in the presence of men than he acknowledges him in the presence of his Father.* We must cut short this sermon. It cannot be finished today without running overtime if I wish to include in this one discourse everything that is left of the text I am expounding. I shall deal with it at another time, that both in word and deed I may please the Church's bridegroom, Jesus Christ our Lord, who is God over all, blessed for ever. Amen.*

SERMON SIXTY-TWO

I. THE MEANING OF THE WALL, AND OF
THE CRANNIES IN WHICH THE DOVE
RESTS. II. HOW THE SOUL MAKES
THESE CRANNIES FOR ITSELF IN THE
WALL OF THE ANGELS, AND HOW IT
HOLLOWS OUT THE ROCK WHICH IS
CHRIST, AS PAUL AND DAVID DID.
III. THE TWO KINDS OF HEAVENLY CON-
TEMPLATION; THOSE SEARCHERS WHOM
GLORY OVERWHELMS, AND THOSE
WHOM IT DOES NOT. IV. HOW THE
CHURCH DWELLS IN THE ROCK THROUGH
ITS PERFECT MEMBERS, IN THE WALL
THROUGH THOSE LESS PERFECT, IN A
TRENCH OF THE EARTH THROUGH ITS
WEAK MEMBERS; THE PERSON AD-
ADDRESSED BY *SHOW ME YOUR FACE,
LET YOUR VOICE SOUND,* AND SO ON.

I. 1. 'MY DOVE IN THE CLEFTS of the rock, in the crannies of the wall.'* The dove finds safe refuge not only in the clefts of the rock, she also finds it in the crannies of the wall. Now if we interpret 'wall' not as a conglomeration of stones but as the communion of saints, let us see if perhaps the crannies of the wall are the places of those angels who fell through

*Sg 2:14

149

pride, leaving behind those empty spaces which are to be filled by men, like ruins repaired by living stones. Hence the apostle Peter says: 'Come to him, to that living stone, and like living stones be yourselves built into spiritual houses'.* Nor do I think it irrelevant if we understand the guardianship of angels to represent a wall in the Lord's vineyard, in the Church of the predestined, since Paul says: 'Are they not all ministering spirits sent forth to serve, for the sake of those who receive the inheritance of salvation?'* And the prophet: 'The angel of the Lord encamps around those who fear him.'* If that is accepted the meaning will be that two things console the Church in the time and place of its pilgrimage:* from the past the memory of Christ's passion, and for the future the thought and confidence of being welcomed among the saints.* In these glimpses of the past and future she contemplates both events with insatiable longing; each aspect is entirely pleasing to her, each a refuge from the distress of troubles and from sorrow.* Her consolation is complete, since she knows not only what to hope for but also the ground of her confidence. Her expectation, founded on the death of Christ, is joyful and undoubting. Why be overawed at the greatness of the reward when she ponders the worthiness of the ransom? How gladly she visits in her mind those clefts through which the ransom of his sacred blood flowed upon her! How gladly she explores the crannies, the refreshing retreats and rooms, which are so many and so diverse in the Father's house,* in

*1 Pet 2:4-5

*Heb 1:14
*Ps 33:8

*Ps 118:54

*Col 1:12

*Pss 31:7,106:39

*Jn 14:2

which he sets up his sons according to the diversity of their merits! But for the moment she does the one thing meanwhile possible, she reposes there in memory, entering now in spirit into the heavenly dwelling that is above. But in time she will fill up those ruins* and dwell in those crannies both in body and mind. Then she will brighten with the presence of her countless members those empty domiciles abandoned by the former inhabitants. No longer will crannies be visible in the wall of heaven, happily restored again to its perfection and completeness. *Ps 109:6*

II. 2. If you prefer, however, let us say that these crannies are not found but rather made by studious and devout minds. How so, you ask? By thought and eager desire. That devout wall, of comparatively soft material, yields to the soul's desire,* yields to pure contemplation, yields to frequent prayer. For 'the just man's prayer pierces the clouds'.* Not that it cleaves the spacious heights of this material atmosphere, of course, as a bird in flight does by the beating of its wings, nor pierces like a sharp sword the dense and lofty dome of the sky; but there are holy heavens, living and rational, which proclaim the glory of God,* which gladly listen to our prayers with gracious acquiescence and, on sensing our devotion, take us affectionately to their hearts as often as we appeal to them with a worthy intention. For 'to him who knocks it will be opened'.* It is therefore within the power of each of us, even during the time of our mortal

Is 26:8

Sir 35:21

Ps 18:1

Mt 7:8

life, to hollow out a place anywhere we will
in the heavenly wall: at our pleasure to visit
the patriarchs now, to salute the prophets
now, to mingle with the assembly of apostles
now. to slip into the choirs of martyrs now,
even to run with all the swiftness of mind that
devotion can inspire through the orders and
dwellings of the blessed spirits, from the
smallest angel to the Cherubim and Seraphim.
And if we stand and knock there where our
attraction has drawn us, inwardly moved as
the Spirit wills,* [the door] will at once be
opened to us,† a cranny will be made amid
the holy mountains—or rather the holy minds
—who will spontaneously and lovingly enfold
us that we may rest with them for a while.
The face and voice of every soul who acts like
this are pleasing to God: the face for its can-
dor, the voice for its praise. For praise and
beauty are in his sight.* And he says to one
thus endowed: 'Show me your face, let your
voice sound in my ears.'* This voice is the
wonder in the mind of the contemplative,
this voice is the giving of thanks. God finds
his delight in these crannies; from them
resounds the voice of gratitude, the voice of
wonder and adoration.

3. Happy the mind which frequently
works at hollowing a place for itself in this
wall, but happier still the one which does so
in the rock! For it is all right to hollow even
in the rock; but for this the mind must have a
keener edge, a more eager purpose, and merits
of a higher order. 'Who is equal to such a calling?'* Evidently he was who said: 'In the
beginning was the Word, and the Word was

*1 Cor 12:11
†Lk 12:36

*Ps 95:6

*Sg 2:14

*2 Cor 2:16

with God, and the Word was God. He was in the beginning with God.'* Does it not seem to you that he had immersed himself in the very inward being of the Word, and from the hidden recesses of his breast had drawn forth the holiest essence of divine wisdom? What about him who imparted wisdom to the perfect, a wisdom wrapt in mystery, which none of the rulers of this age understood?* Passing through the first and second heavens by his keen but holy curiosity, did the devout scrutinizer not gain at last this wisdom from the third?* But he has not hidden it from us, he has faithfully delivered it to the capable in well-chosen words. But he also heard unutterable words that he was not permitted to speak, at least not to men, for he spoke them to himself and to God.* Imagine therefore that God, trying to console the tender love of Paul, says to him: 'Why do you worry because the human hearing cannot grasp your thought? "Let your voice sound in my ears."'* That is: if what you perceive may not be revealed to mortals, be nevertheless consoled, because your voice can delight the ears of God.' You see this holy soul now sober through love for us, then transported in pure attachment to God!* Look too at holy David, whether he himself is not the man about whom he says to God as if about another: 'For the thought of a man will offer you praise, and the residue of his thought will be a feastday for you.'* As much of prophetic thought as could come through the prophet's word and example, therefore, he at once disclosed in publicly praising the Lord and declaring it among the

*Jn 1:1-2

*1 Cor 2:6-8

*2 Cor 12:2

*2 Cor 12:4

*Sg 2:14

*2 Cor 5:13

*Ps 75:11

people; the residue he reserved for himself and for God, holding festival together in gladness and rejoicing.* This then is what he wished to convey to us in the verse quoted. Whatever was appropriate in all that he was able to learn from the mystery of wisdom by an eager and inquiring mind, he imparted for the salvation of men by zealous preaching; the residue which the people could not grasp he employed in praising God with festive joy. As you see, there is no less to holy contemplation when all that cannot be used for the instruction of the people becomes a sweet and gracious praise of God.*

III. 4. This being so, it is obvious that there are two kinds of contemplation: one concerns the state and happiness and glory of the heavenly city, in which either by activity or by repose a great crowd of its citizens are engaged; the other concerns the majesty, the eternity and the divinity of the king himself. The former exists in the wall, the latter in the rock. The more difficult the hollowing in the former the sweeter the yield; nor need one fear the scriptural threat about the scrutinizer of majesty.* Just bring to it an eye that is pure and simple,* and you will not be overwhelmed by glory but led into it*—unless you seek your own glory, not God's. For each person is weighed down not by God's glory but by his own, when by his bent for his own he cannot raise to God's a head burdened by cupidity. But let us rid ourselves of this and excavate confidently in the rock where the hidden treasures of wisdom and knowledge

Ps 44:16

Ps 146:1

Prov 25:27
Lk 11:34
Prov 25:27

are stored.* If you still hesitate listen to the   **Col 2:3*
rock itself: 'They who do things in me shall
not sin.'* 'Who will give me wings like a dove,   **Sir 24:30*
and I will fly away and be at rest.'* The meek   **Ps 54:7*
and the simple find rest* there where the   **Mt 11:29*
deceitful, the proud, the seekers of vain-
glory are trodden down.* The Church is a   **Gal 5:26*
dove and therefore is at rest. A dove because
innocent, because mourning.* A dove, I say,   **Cf. Is 59:11*
because she receives the implanted word
meekly.* And she reposes in the Word, that is,   **Jas 1:21*
in the rock, for the rock is the word.*   **1 Cor 10:4*
The Church dwells therefore in the clefts of
the rock. Through them she gazes at and
beholds the glory of her bridegroom. Nor
is she overwhelmed by glory because she does
not arrogate it to herself. She is not overwhelmed because she is a scrutinizer not of
God's majesty but of his will. What touches
upon his majesty, she does indeed sometimes
dare to contemplate it, but in admiration, not
in scrutiny. But if at times she is even rapt
toward it in ecstasy, this is the finger of God
deigning to raise man up,* not the brashness   **Ex 8, Lk 11:20*
of a man insolently intruding on the lofty
things of God. For when the apostle recalls
being rapt he apologizes for its daring;* what   **2 Cor 12:2*
other mortal then would presume to involve
himself by his own attempts at an awesome
scrutiny of the divine majesty, what insolent
contemplative would force his way into those
dread secrets? The scrutinizers of majesty
described as invaders are not, I think then,
those who are rapt into it, but those who
force their way in. They are understandably
overwhelmed by glory.

5. Scrutinizing God's majesty is then a thing to fear; but scrutinizing his will is as safe as it is dutiful. Why should I not tirelessly concentrate on searching into the mystery of his glorious will, which I know I must obey in all things? Sweet is the glory which has no source but the contemplation of sweetness itself, than the vision of the riches of his good-ness and the multitude of his mercies.* The glory we have seen is the glory of the Father's Only-begotten.* For whatever glory has been manifested in this way is totally kind, truly paternal. This glory will not oppress me,* though I lean toward it with all my strength; it will rather impress itself upon me. 'And we all, with unveiled face, beholding the glory of the Lord, are being transformed into his like-ness from one degree of glory to another; for this comes from the Lord who is the Spirit.'* We are transformed when we are conformed, God forbid that a man presume to be con-formed to God in the glory of his majesty rather than in the modesty of his will. My glory is this,* to hear it one day said of me: 'I have found a man according to my own heart.'* The heart of the Bridegroom is the Father's heart. And how describe this? Christ said: 'Be merciful, even as your Father is merciful.'* This is the form he desires to see when he says to the Church: 'Let me see your face',* the form of love and gentleness. Let her raise this [face] with complete trust to the Rock, whose likeness she bears. 'Look to him', [the psalmist] says, 'and be enlightened, so your faces shall never be ashamed.'* How can the humble [face] be put to shame by the

*Ex 34:6,
Rom 2:4

*Jn 1:14

*Prov 25:27

*2 Cor 3:18

*2 Cor 1:12

*Acts 13:22

*Lk 6:36

*Sg 2:14

*Ps 33:6

humble [person], the holy by one who is dutiful, the modest by one who is meek? The bride's pure face will recoil from the purity of the Rock no more than virtue will from virtue, or light from light.

IV. 6. But since in the meantime the Church as a whole cannot draw near to make clefts in the rock—for it is not within the power of everybody in the Church to examine the mysteries of the divine will* or of themselves to pierce the depths of God*—therefore she is shown to dwell not only in the clefts of the rock but also in the crannies of the wall. Accordingly she dwells in the clefts of the rock through her perfect [members] who by their purity of conscience dare to explore and penetrate into the secrets of wisdom, and can achieve this by their keenness of mind. As for the crannies of the wall, those who of themselves are unable or will not presume to dig in the rock, let them dig in the wall, content to gaze mentally upon the glory of the saints. If even this is not possible to someone, let him place before him Jesus and him crucified,* that without effort on his part he may dwell in those clefts of the rock at whose hollowing he has not labored.* The Jews labored at them, and He will enter the labors of an unbeliever to make a believer of him. Nor must he who has been invited to enter dread a rebuff. 'Enter into the rock', says [Isaiah], 'and hide in the hollowed ground from the face of the terror of the Lord, and from the glory of his majesty.'* To the soul who is still weak and sluggish, the one

*Eph 1:9
*1 Cor 2:10

*1 Cor 2:2

*Jn 4:38

*Is 2:10

*Lk 16:3
who confesses with the gospel that he is unable to dig and ashamed to beg,* there is shown a hollow in the ground where he may hide until he grows strong and vigorous enough to hollow out for himself clefts in the rock through which he may enter into the inward being of the Word by the energy and purity of his mind.

7. And if we understand that the hollow in the ground is referred to [in the words]: *Ps 21:17 'they have dug my hands and my feet',* we cannot doubt that the wounded soul who abides there will quickly regain health. What greater cure for the wounds of conscience and for purifying the mind's acuity that to persevere in meditation on the wounds of Christ? Indeed until he has been perfectly purifed and healed I do not see how anyone can suitably listen to the words: 'Let me see your *Sg 2:14 face, let me hear your voice.'* How can anyone dare show his face or raise his voice if he is ordered to hide? He was told to 'hide in *Is 2:10 the hollowed ground'.* Why? Because without facial beauty he is not fit to be seen. He will not be fit to be seen as long as he is not equipped for seeing. But when by dwelling in the hollow in the ground he will so have succeeded in healing his inward vision that he can *2 Cor 3:18 gaze on the glory of God with unveiled face,* then at last, pleasing both in voice and face, he will confidently proclaim what he sees. The face that can focus on the brightness of God must of necessity be pleasing. Nor could it accomplish this unless it were itself bright and pure, transformed into the very image of the brightness it beholds. Otherwise it would

recoil through sheer unlikeness, driven back by the unaccustomed splendor. When a pure [soul] can therefore gaze on the pure truth, the Bridegroom himself will want to look on his face, and then to hear his voice.

8. He shows how greatly the preaching of the truth with a pure mind pleases him when immediately he says: 'for your voice is sweet.'* That the voice does not please if the face displeases he shows when he adds at once: 'and your face comely.' What is the comeliness of the inner face if not purity? The one was found attractive in many without the preaching of the word; the other without it in no one. Truth does not show itself nor Wisdom entrust itself to the impure. How can they speak of that which they have not seen? 'We speak of what we know', [John] said, 'and we bear witness to what we have seen.'* Go then and dare to bear witness to what you have not seen, to preach what you do not know. Do you ask whom I call impure? Anyone who looks for human praise, who does not deliver the Gospel without charge,* who preaches for a livelihood, who considers godliness a means of gain,* who does not work for the [spiritual] fruit but for contribution. Such are the impure; and though lacking the power to perceive the truth because of their impurity, they presume to preach it. Why do you act so hastily? Why not wait for the light? Why presume to do the work of the light before [you see] the light? It is useless for you to rise before light.* Light is purity, light is the love which does not insist on its own way.* Let this take

*Sg 2:14

*Jn 3:11

*1 Cor 9:18
*1 Tim 6:5

*Ps 126:2
*1 Cor 13:5

*Ps 100:5

*Ps 49:16

*Rom 2:21

*Rom 9:5

the lead and your tongue will not move like an unsteady foot. The truth is not visible to the haughty eye,* it is manifest to the sincere. Truth does not withold its vision from the pure of heart, and so fail to be proclaimed. 'To the sinner God says: "what right have you to recite my statutes, or take my covenant on your lips?" '* Many, slighting this purity, endeavor to speak before they see. They have seriously erred, ignorant of what they are saying or of what they claim, incurred shameful derision as those who teach others while failing to teach themselves.* Through your prayers may we be always preserved from these two evils by the Church's Bridegroom, our Lord Jesus Christ, who is God over all, blessed for ever.* Amen.

SERMON SIXTY-THREE

I. THE VINEYARD WHICH THE FOXES
DESTROY. II. ONLY A WISE PERSON HAS
A VINEYARD WITH VINE, YOUNG SHOOTS,
WINE; THE FOXES WHO DESTROY IT, AND
HOW THEY ARE CAUGHT. III. THE
FRUITS OF THE VINE, THE NOVICES AS
FLOWERS, THE DANGER FOR THESE
FLOWERS

I. 1. 'CATCH US THE LITTLE FOXES that destroy the vines; for our vine has flowered.'* Obviously the trip to the vineyard was no waste of time, since foxes were discovered there destroying it. That is what the literal meaning says. But what is the spiritual? First of all we must totally reject in our interpretation the common and familiar meaning of the text as absurd and insipid and clearly unworthy of inclusion in holy and authentic Scripture. One may, of course, be so stupid, so mentally dull, as to think he is getting an important lesson here, like one of this world's children,* on how to care for earthly possessions, to protect and defend his vineyard against the incursions of wild animals, lest he forfeit the enjoyment of the wine, in which is debauchery,* while labor and expense are wasted. A

*Sg 2:15

*Lk 16:8, 20:34

*Eph 5:18

161

mighty loss indeed, if we are to read the holy
book with such great care, such veneration
that we may learn from it to guard our vineyard against foxes, for fear we should have
vainly emptied our purses for its cultivation
by being remiss in caring for it. You are not
so cloddish, so devoid of spiritual grace, as to
understand it in this carnal fashion. Let us
therefore look for the spiritual meaning. We
do indeed find there, by sound understanding
and worthy sense, both flowering vines and
destructive foxes, in whose capture and removal we shall be profitably and becomingly
employed. Can you doubt that souls must be
guarded with far greater vigilance than crops,
that far more watchfulness is required in
warding off the spiritual forces of evil* than
in catching cunning little foxes?

*Eph 6:12

2.   It is up to me now to explain the spiritual meaning of the vines and foxes. It will be
your job, my sons, for you, each of you to
provide for his own vineyard, when he appre-
hends from my words the situations and
dangers he must be especially wary of. To a
wise man the vineyard means his life, his
soul, his conscience. And the wise man will
tolerate nothing in himself that is unculti-
vated or gone to waste. Not so the fool: with
him you will find everything neglected, everything lying about, everything filthy and un-
cared for. The fool has no vines. How can
there be a vineyard where there is no sign of
planting, no sign of cultivation anywhere?
The fool's whole life bristles with briars and
thistles—some vineyard! There may once have
been one but there no longer is, reduced as it

is to a wilderness.* Where is the vine of
virtue? Where the grapes of good works?
Where the wine of spiritual gladness? 'I passed
by the field of a sluggard, by the vineyard of a
man without sense,' it says, 'and lo, it was all
overgrown with thorns, the ground was
covered with nettles, and the stone wall was
broken down.'* You are hearing the wise man
mock at the fool because, by neglecting the
endowments of nature and the gifts of grace
which he had received in the cleansing water
of rebirth,* he has reduced his very own first
vineyard (which God, not man, had planted)*
to something that is no vineyard. Besides,
there can be no vineyard where there is no
life. The fool may be alive, but to me it is
death rather than life. How can life exist with
barrenness? Isn't a withered and barren tree
considered dead? Strewn branches are also
dead. 'He killed their vines with hail',* said
[the psalmist], showing that those condemned to barrenness are deprived of life.
And so the fool, since he lives to no purpose,
is dead even as he lives.*

*Jer 50:13

*Prov 24:30-31

*Tit 3:5
*Lk 20:9

*Ps 77:47

*1 Tim 5:6

II. 3. Only of the wise man, who possesses
life, can it then be said that he has, or better,
is, a vineyard. He is a fruitful tree in God's
house,* and because of this living wood.
Indeed the very wisdom through which a man
is, and is called, wise, is a tree of life to those
who lay hold of her.* Why should he who
lays hold of her not live? He does live, but by
faith. The wise man is a just man, and the just
man lives by faith.* And if the soul of the just
man is the abode of wisdom,* then he who is

*Ps 51:10

*Prov 3:18

*Rom 1:17
*Prov 12:23 (LXX)

just is wise. Therefore whether you call him just or wise, he never lives without a vineyard because he is never otherwise than alive. His life is his vineyard. And the just man's vineyard is good, or rather the just man is a good vineyard; his virtue is like the vine, his deeds like the branches, his wine the witness of his conscience, his tongue the wine-press. The one thing we are proud of, said [St Paul], is the witness of our conscience.* Do you see how nothing is in vain for the wise man? His discourse, his thoughts, his manner of life, his whole conduct, is it not all God's farm, God's building,* the vineyard of the Lord of Sabaoth?* Can any of it be lost to him, when its leaves do not fade?*

4. On the other hand, such a vineyard is never free from infestation and infiltrations. For 'where goods abound, nibblers abound'.* The wise man will be no less concerned to guard his vineyard than to cultivate it, he will not allow it to be a prey to foxes. The worst fox is the hidden slanderer, but just as bad is the smooth-tongued sycophant. A wise person will beware of these. He will strive, as much as he can, to catch those who do such things, but to catch them by kindness and courtesies, by wholesome advice and by praying to God for them.* He will not cease to heap coals of fire* on the head of the maligner, on the head of the sycophant until—if possible—he banishes envy from the heart of the one, hypocrisy from that of the other, fulfilling the command of the Bridegroom: 'Catch us the little foxes that destroy the vines.'* Surely someone caught with cheeks all red, and

*2 Cor 1:12

*1 Cor 3:9
*Is 5:7
*Ps 1:3

*Qo 5:10

*Acts 12:5
*Rom 12:20

*Sg 2:15

blushing his own judgment, will seem to you a witness to his own undoing and penitence, either because of his hate for a person so deserving of love or because he loved in words or talk alone one by whom, he realized too late, he was loved in deed and in truth?* Caught obviously he is, and caught for the Lord according to his distinct command: 'catch [them] for us'. Would that I could catch all who oppose me without cause,* and either restore them to or acquire them for Christ! Yes, 'shame and disgrace be on those who seek my life; may those who wish me evil retreat in dismay'!* But let me be found submissive to the Bridegroom, that I too may catch the foxes, not for me but for him. But let us go back to where we began that our exposition may proceed with due sequence.

5. 'Catch us the little foxes that destroy the vines.'* This text has a moral import, and taking it in a moral sense we have already shown that these spiritual vineyards signify spiritual men within whom all things are cultivated, all things are germinating, bearing fruit and bringing forth the spirit of salvation. What was said of the kingdom of God we can equally say of these vineyards of the Lord of hosts*—that they are within us.† We read in the Gospel that the kingdom will be given to a people who will produce its fruits.* St Paul enumerates these: 'The fruit of the Spirit is love, joy, peace, patience, kindness, goodness, forbearance, gentleness, faithfulness, modesty, self-control, chastity.'* These fruits indicate our progress. They are pleasing to the Bridegroom because he takes care of us.* Is

*1 Jn 3:18

*Ps 7:8

*Ps 34:4, 69:4

*Sg 2:15

*Is 5:7
†Lk 17:21

*Mt 21:43

*Gal 5:22-23

*1 Pet 5:7

1 Cor 9:9

God concerned about bushes?* The Man–God loves men, not trees, and counts our progress as his own fruits. Unflaggingly he watches for their season, smiles when they appear, and anxiously strives that we should not lose them when they do appear; or rather that he should not lose them, for we are as dear to him as he is. With foresight then he orders that the cunning little foxes be caught for him, lest they pilfer the immature fruits: 'Catch us the little foxes,' he says, 'that destroy the vines.' And if someone were to object: 'Your fears are premature—the time of fruiting has not yet come', he answers: 'it is not so, already "our vineyard has flowered".'*

Sg 2:15

Between flowers and fruit there is no delay: while the flowers are falling the fruits are budding forth, they begin to show at once.

Heb 9:9

6.   That parable is for our times.* Do you see these novices? They came recently, they were converted recently. We cannot say of them that 'our vineyard has flowered': it is flowering. What you see appear in them at the moment is the blossom; the time of fruiting has not yet come. Their new way of life, their recent adoption of a better life—these are blossoms. They have assumed a disciplined appearance, a proper deportment in their whole body. What can be seen of them is pleasing, I admit: One notices less attention to painstaking care of the body and of dress; they speak less, their faces are more cheerful, their looks more modest, their movements more correct. But since these are new beginnings, the flowers must be judged by their very novelty, and a promise of fruits rather

than the fruits themselves. For you, my young sons, I do not fear the cunning of the foxes, who are known to hunger for the fruits, not for the blossoms. The threat to you is from elsewhere. What I dread for the blossoms is not theft but blight from the cold. The north wind is unwelcome to me, and the morning frosts that are wont to destroy the early blossoms and deprive us of fruit. Hence any harm to you threatens from the north.* **Jer 1:14* 'Who will endure the cold?'* If this cold once **Ps 147:17* penetrates the soul when (as so often happens) the soul is neglectful and the spirit asleep and if no one (God forbid) is there to curb it, then it reaches into the soul's interior, descends to the depths of the heart and the recesses of the mind, paralyses the affections, obstructs the paths of counsel, unsteadies the light of judgment, fetters the liberty of the spirit, and soon—as appears to bodies sick with fever—a rigor of the mind takes over: vigor slackens, energies grow languid, repugnance for austerity increases, fear of poverty disquiets, the soul shrivels, grace is withdrawn, time means boredom, reason is lulled to sleep, the spirit is quenched,* the **1 Thess 5:19* fresh fervor wanes away, a fastidious lukewarmness weighs down, brotherly love grows cold,* pleasure attracts, security is a trap, **Mt 24:12* old habits return. Can I say more? The law is cheated, justice is rejected, what is right is outlawed, the fear of the Lord is abandoned.* **Job 6:14* Shamelessness finally gets free rein. There comes that rash leap, so dishonorable, so disgraceful, so full of ignominy and confusion; a leap from the heights into the abyss, from

the court-yard to the dung-heap, from the
throne to the sewer, from heaven to the mud,
from the cloister to the world, from paradise
to hell. Now is not the time to reveal the
source and origin of this plague, or the skills
by which to avoid it, or the power by which it
may be overcome; there is another place for
that. Now let us pursue what we began with.

7. We turn back our discussion to those
who are more advanced and more stable, to
the vineyard which has already flowered,
whose flowers need no longer fear the cold,
but whose fruits are not safe from the foxes.
One must say more plainly what the spiritual
significance of these foxes is, why they are
called small, especially why they are ordered
to be caught and not driven away or killed.
And the various kinds of these animals must
be introduced, that by knowing them better
listeners may be on their guard—not however
in this sermon so I do not weary you, and so
that the freshness of our devotion may be
preserved in the grace and praise of the glory
of the Church's great Bridegroom, our Lord
Jesus Christ, who is God over all, blessed

Rom 9:5
for ever.* Amen.

SERMON SIXTY-FOUR

I. THE DIFFERENT KINDS OF FOXES,
THAT IS, OF SUBTLE TEMPTATIONS, OF
WHICH THERE ARE FOUR. II. WHY WE
ARE ORDERED TO CAPTURE, RATHER
THAN KILL OR DRIVE AWAY. THE FOXES
AND WHY THEY ARE CALLED LITTLE.
III. THE FOXES ARE HERETICS. HOW THE
BRIDEGROOM HAS TOLD US TO CAPTURE
THEM.

I. 1. I STAND BY MY PROMISE: 'Catch us the little foxes that spoil the vines, for our vines are in flower.'* These foxes represent temptations. Now it is necessary that temptations come,* for who shall receive a crown of victory unless he has contended according to the rules?* And how shall they contend if there is no-one to oppose them? When you come to serve God, then, stand in awe and prepare your soul for temptation,* certain that all who wish to live a godly life in Christ must suffer persecution.* Now there are different kinds of temptation, corresponding to different times [in our lives]. At the beginning of our course, when we are like tender flowers on young plants, a sharp frost attacks us openly, as I described in my last sermon,* and I have warned

*Sg 2:15

*Matt 18:7

*2 Tim 2:5

*Sir 2:1
*2 Tim 3:12

*Sermon 63.6-7
Ps 15:11

169

beginners to beware of this bane. Yet the powerful enemies of good do not dare openly to oppose the proficient, who have made some progress in sanctity, but they lie in wait for them in secret, like cunning little foxes, wearing the likeness of virtues, whereas they are really vices. How many, for instance, have I known who, at the beginning of life's journey,* started out all right on the paths of righteousness* and were making serene progress towards goodness when, for shame! they suffer the humiliation of being tripped up by these little foxes, and too late they grieve for the fruits of virtue which have been choked in them.

*Ps 15:11
*Prov 2:8

2. I have seen a man running his course well,* and then this thought occurs to him—is it not a little fox?—'If I were at home', he says, 'I could share with so many of my brothers, kinsfolk, and acquaintances the good I here enjoy alone.* They love me, and would readily agree with me when I appeal to them. To what purpose is this waste?* I will go to them, and by saving many of them I shall save myself also. There is nothing to fear in a change of environment. As long as I am doing good, it does not matter where I am, although, of course, it is no doubt better to be where I may live a more useful life.' Need I say more? He goes, poor wretch, not so much an exile returning home as a dog returning to his vomit,* and he is destroyed. Unhappy man, he loses his own soul without saving anyone else's. Surely this is a little fox—the vain hope of winning the souls of others? You can find one instance after another

*Gal 5:7

*Lk 16:28

*Matt 26:8

*2 Pet 2:22

like this for yourselves from your own experience if you take the trouble.

3. Do you want me to show you yet another? I will, and I will describe a third and a fourth as well if I find you watchful* and eager to catch those, of whatever kind, which you may notice in your own vineyard. It sometimes happens that a man who is making good progress feels himself bedewed with heavenly grace to an extraordinary degree, and is possessed by a desire to preach, not indeed to his relatives and friends—you remember the saying 'Immediately I conferred not with flesh and blood'*—but to all and sundry, as though that were a purer, more fruitful and more powerful procedure. He is acting with great caution. No doubt he is afraid of incurring the prophet's curse if he holds back from the people the grain which he received in secret,* and is afraid of acting contrary to the Gospel if he does not proclaim from the housetop what he hears whispered.* This too is a fox, even more dangerous than the last, because its coming is less obvious; but I will catch it for you. First, Moses says 'You shall not plough with the first-born or your bull'.* This Paul interprets as: 'Not a new convert, lest being lifted up with pride he fall into the condemnation of the devil',* and again, 'A man does not take this honor upon himself, but is called by God, as was Aaron',* and yet again: 'How can men preach unless they are sent?'* Now we know that the duty of a monk is not to teach but to weep.* Of these and like considerations I weave my net and catch the fox so that it

Lk 12:37

Gal 1:16

Prov 11:26

Matt 10:27

Deut 15:19

1 Tim 3:6

Heb 5:4
Rom 10:15
*St Jerome,
Contra Vigilantium 15; PL
23:367A.*

may not spoil the vine. They make it quite clear that it is not expedient for a monk to preach in public, nor is it seemly for a novice, nor proper for anyone unless he is expressly sent. What devastation of the conscience to fly in the face of all these three! Therefore if any suggestion of this kind presents itself to you, whether it arises from your own mind or is suggested by an evil spirit,* you must recognize it as a cunning fox, evil disguised as good.

*Ps 77:49

4. Look at another [example]. How many fervent souls have been drawn from their monasteries by the attraction of the solitary life,* and have then become lukewarm and have been spewed forth,* or if they have remained, have become slack and dissolute, violating the law of the hermit? A little fox has plainly been at work when such havoc has been caused in the vineyard! It is the destruction of a man's life and integrity. He supposed that the solitary life would produce the fruits of the Spirit in much greater abundance than the common life, where he had experienced, so he thought, only ordinary grace. The idea seemed to him a good one, but the outcome showed that it was more like a destructive fox.

*Rom 12:11
*Rev 3:16

5. Now I must mention a matter which frequently causes us serious trouble: the excessive and superstitious abstinence of some among us, which makes them a burden to themselves and everyone else. How can such discord do other than cause the destruction of the consciences of those concerned, and, as far as is in their power, the devastation of this great vine which the right hand of the Lord has

planted, by destroying the unity of all of
you?* 'Woe to the man by whom the   *Ps 79:16*
offence comes!* Whoever causes one of these   *Matt 18:7*
little ones to stumble'*—what follows is hard,   *Matt 18:6*
but how much harder a fate does the man
deserve who causes so great and holy a multi-
tude to stumble! Whoever he is,* he will bear   *Gal 5:10*
his judgment, and it will be very severe. But of
this [I will speak] another time.

II. 6. Now let us consider what the Bridegroom said about these cunning little animals
that spoil the vines. They are little, I would
say, not because they have little malice, but
because of their subtlety. This kind of creature
is indeed cunning by nature, and exceedingly
quick to do damage in secret, and it may, I
think, be most appropriate to consider them
as representing certain subtle vices cloaked in
the likeness of virtues. I have already given a
brief description of their nature and cited a
few examples. They can do no damage at all
except by falsely representing themselves as
virtues, because of their very likeness to virtues. For they are either the vain thoughts
of men* or the promptings of Satan's evil   *Ps 93:11*
angels,* who disguise themselves as angels of   *Ps 77:49*
light,* making ready their arrows in the   *2 Cor 11:14*
quiver*—that is in secret—to shoot in the dark   *Ps 10:2*
at the upright in heart.† That, I think, is why   †Ps 10:3*
they are called little, for while other vices
show themselves as it were in bodily form,
this kind are not easily recognized because of
their subtlety. They cannot easily be avoided
except by the perfect and the experienced,
and by such as have the eyes of their souls

*Eph 1:18

*1 Cor 12:10

*2 Cor 2:11

*Job 5:13

*Matt 22:15

enlightened* for the discernment of good and evil, and particularly for the discernment of spirits,* so that they can say with the Apostle Paul: 'We are not ignorant of the designs of Satan'* or of his thoughts. Perhaps it is for this reason that the Bridegroom has given orders that they are not to be exterminated or driven away or killed, but caught. Cunning little beasts of this kind must obviously be watched with the utmost vigilance and caution, and so trapped, that is caught in the toils of their own subtlety.* Then, when their deception is made known and their falsity uncovered, it can truly be said that the little fox that destroys the vine has been caught. Thus we say that a man is trapped in his speech, as you find in the Gospel: 'The Pharisees came together to trap Jesus in his speech.'*

7. This is why the Bridegroom gives orders that the little foxes who spoil the vines are to be caught, that is trapped, overcome, and brought out into the open. This kind of pest is the only one with the peculiarity, that once recognized it can do no harm; if it is recognized it is conquered. Who but a madman would knowingly and consciously put his foot into a trap if he knew it was there. It is enough, then, for this kind to be caught, that is, discovered and brought into the light of day, since for them to be seen is to perish. It is not so with other vices, for they attack openly, and their damage is done openly. They ensnare even those who are aware of them and overcome even those who resist them, and that by force, not by guile. When we are dealing with beasts of this kind who

rage openly, we have not to flush them out, but to bring them under control. It is only these little foxes, these great deceivers, whom it suffices to bring into the light of day and catch in the toils of their cunning.* Once they are recognized they can do no harm—but they do have holes. This is why we are commanded to catch these foxes, and why they are described as little. Or perhaps they are so called because it is by careful observation in the early stages, while they are still small, that you may catch vices in time and prevent them from growing larger and doing greater damage, besides becoming more difficult to catch.

*Matt 8:20

III. 8. If we continue the allegory, taking vines to represent christian congregations, and foxes heresies, or rather heretics themselves, the interpretation is simple: heretics are to be caught rather than driven away. They are to be caught, I repeat, not by force of arms but by arguments by which their errors may be refuted. They themselves, if it can be done, are to be reconciled with the Catholic [Church] and brought back to the true faith. This is His will,* that all men should be saved and brought to the knowledge of the truth.* This is what he shows us when he says not simply 'Catch the foxes', but 'Catch us the foxes'. It is for himself and his bride, that is the Catholic [Church], that he orders these foxes to be apprehended when he says 'Catch us the foxes'. So if an experienced and well-instructed churchman undertakes to debate with a heretic, he should

*Jn 6:39-40

*1 Tim 2:4

direct his intention to convincing him of the error of his ways in such a way as to convert him, bearing in mind the saying of the Apostle James, that anyone who causes a sinner to be converted from the error of his ways will save his soul from death and cover a multitude of sins.* But if he will not be converted or convinced even after a first and second admonition, then, according to the Apostle, he is to be shunned* as one who is completely perverted. Consequently I think it better that he should be driven away or even bound rather than be allowed to spoil the vines.

9. Let it not be supposed, however, that it is a small and unimportant thing for a man to vanquish a heretic and refute his heresies, making a clear and open distinction between shadows and reality and exposing the fallacies of false teaching by plain and irrefutable reasoning in such a way as to bring into captivity a depraved mind which had set itself up against the knowledge revealed by God.* The man who has done this has in fact caught the fox, though not to his salvation, and he has caught it for the Bride and Bridegroom, though in a different way. For even though the heretic was not raised up from the error of his ways, the Church has been strengthened in faith,* and without doubt the Bridegroom rejoices in the progress of the Bride. 'The joy of the Lord is our strength.'* He who has deigned to unite himself with us does not look upon our advantage as something foreign to himself, for he orders the foxes to be caught, not for himself, but for us along with him. Notice that he says 'for us'. What

*Jas 5:20

*Tit 3:10

*2 Cor 10:5

*Col 2:7

*Neh 8:10

gracious condescension! Do you not think
that he is speaking as the father of a family,
in that he keeps nothing for himself, but has
everything in common with his wife and
children and household? He who speaks is
indeed God, yet it is not as God that he
speaks, but as a Bridegroom.

10. 'Catch us the foxes.' You see how he
speaks, as though to equals—he who has no
equal. He could have said 'me', but he preferred to say 'us', for he delights in companionship. What sweetness! What grace! What
mighty love! Can it be that the Highest of
all is made one with all? Who has brought this
about? Love has brought this about, without
regard for its own dignity, strong in affection
and efficacious in persuasion. What could be
more violent? Love prevails even with God.
What could be so non-violent? It is love. What
force is there, I ask, which advances so violently
towards victory, yet is so unresisting to violence? For he emptied himself, so that you
might know that it was the fulness of love
which was outpoured,* that his loftiness was   *Phil 2:7
laid low and that his unique nature made to be
your fellow. With whom, O wonderful Bridegroom, have you such familiar friendship?
'Catch them for us,' he says. For whom, besides
you? For the Church of the Gentiles? She is
made up of mortals and sinners. What she is,
we know; but who are you,* so devoted   *Jn 1:19
to the ethiopian woman,* so eager a lover?   *Num 12:1
Assuredly not a second Moses, but a greater
than Moses. Are you not he who is the
fairest of the children of men?* I have   *Ps 44:3,Wis 7:26
said too little. You are the brightness of

eternal life, the splendor and image of the being of God, God over all, blessed for ever.* Amen.

SERMON SIXTY-FIVE

I. BY THE WORD FOXES ARE MEANT
THE NEW HERETICS, ESPECIALLY THE
TOULOUSANS, WHO HIDE THEIR SECT
BY PERJURY. II. HOW THESE FOXES
ARE DETECTED WHILE COHABITING
WOMEN. III. HOW THESE FOXES ARE
CAPTURED WITHOUT SCANDAL IF
POSSIBLE.

I. 1. I HAVE PREACHED two sermons to you on the same verse, and have a third prepared, if you are not weary of listening. I think it is necessary to preach it. As far as our domestic vine is concerned—which is what you are—I think that in two sermons I have given you sufficient warning to protect you from the wiles of three kinds of foxes, namely flatterers, detractors, and seducers of the spirit, who are skilled and practised in representing evil in the guise of good. But it is not so with the vineyard of the Lord—that one, I mean, which encompasses the world, of which we are a part—a vine great beyond measure, planted by the Lord,* bought with his blood, fertilized by grace and made fruitful by his Spirit.* And the more I dwell on our domestic matters, the less use I am in matters of general

*Ps 79:16
*1 Cor 3:6

179

concern. I am greatly troubled for that vine
when I see the multitude of those who would
spoil it, the small number of its defenders, and
the difficulty of its defence. The reason for
this is the subtlety of the attack. For although
the Church has always, even from the beginning, had its foxes, they have all been
quickly discovered and caught. A heretic
would dispute in the open, for the desire
for an open victory is the strongest motive of
a heretic. Then he would surrender; so those
foxes were easily caught. And even if after the
truth was established a heretic remained in
the darkness of his obduracy, languishing
alone in his bonds in outer darkness, even
then the fox would be accounted as caught,
for the impiety stood condemned, and the
impious one was cast out, his life now to be
an empty show, bearing no fruit. Hence-
forward, in the words of the Prophet Hosea,

Hos 9:14   he had dry breasts and a miscarrying womb,*
for an error publicly refuted does not spring
up again, and falsehood revealed does not
take root.

2. What shall we do with those foxes, the
most malicious of all, who would rather
inflict injury than win a victory in open
fight? How shall they be caught, when they do
not even allow themselves to be seen, but
prefer to creep about like snakes? The one
aim of all heretics has always been to gain
renown for the remarkable extent of their
knowledge. But this particular heresy is more
tainted by malice and subtlety than all the
rest, for it feeds upon the destruction of
others and is not concerned with its own

renown. Instructed, I think, by the examples
[of heresies] of old, which could not escape
once they were discovered, but were caught
right away, it is careful to keep secret the
nature of its wickedness. The less suspicion it
arouses, the more freedom it is allowed.* *1 Thess 2:7*
Then these men have appointed hiding-places
for themselves, as it is written: 'They hold fast
to their evil purpose.'* 'Swear, or be foresworn, *Ps 63:6*
but do not betray the secret.' But at other
times they will not consent to swear at all,
even in the slightest degree, because of the
saying of the Evangelist [Matthew]: 'Swear
not at all, neither by heaven nor by earth.'* *Matt 5:34-5*
and so on. O foolish and slow of heart,* filled *Lk 24:25*
with the spirit of the Pharisees, straining at a
gnat and swallowing a camel!* You may not *Matt 23:24*
swear, yet you may be forsworn? Or are both
permissible in this one instance? In what
passage of the Gospels, not even one iota of
which you falsely boast you do not pass
over,* do you find this exception? Obviously *Matt 5:18*
you have superstitious scruples about taking
an oath, but in your wickedness you take
perjury lightly. What perversity! What was
given me as a counsel of perfection, 'Swear
not', that is, they observe as minutely as if it
were a positive command; but committing
perjury, which is forbidden by natural law
(which is unchangeable) they dismiss at will as
unimportant. 'No,' they say, 'we must not
reveal our secret.' As though it were to the
glory of God not to reveal teaching.* Are *Prov 25:2*
they jealous for the glory of God? I think it
more likely that they would blush to expose
their secret, knowing it to be shameful. For it

is said that they practise unspeakable obscenities in private; just so the hinder parts of foxes stink.

3. But I say nothing of what they would deny; let them answer only the direct evidence. Do they take care to follow the Gospel precept not to give what is holy to dogs, or *Matt 7:6* not to cast pearls before swine?* When they dismiss everyone within the Church as dogs and swine, is this not an open admission that they themselves are not within the Church? They consider that their secret, whatever it is, should be kept from everyone, without exception, who does not belong to their sect. Yet although this may be their opinion, they will not admit it, and they run in every direc-*1 Cor 11:19* tion to avoid discovery;* but there will be no *1 Thess 5:3* escape for them.*

Rom 12:3 II. Tell me, O man wise beyond propriety* and foolish beyond description, that secret which you keep hidden—is it of God or not? If it is, why do you not expose it to his glory? For it is the glory of God to reveal teaching.[1] If it is not, why do you put faith in something not of God, unless you are a heretic? Let them either disclose their secret to the glory of God or else admit that it is not a mystery of God and cease to deny that they are heretics; or at least let them recognize that they are openly hostile to the glory of God, since they refuse to disclose what they

1. Prov 25:2 (LXX, Vulgate, and all English translations have the opposite sense. St Gregory, Homilies on Ezekiel 1,6, has it in this sense, however. See Tobit 12:7—trans.)

know would be to his glory. The truth of
Scripture states beyond question: 'It is the
glory of kings to conceal a matter, but the
glory of God to reveal teaching.'* Are you   *Prov 25:2*
unwilling to reveal it? Then you are unwilling
to glorify God. But perhaps you do not
accept this text? This must be so, for men like
you assert that they are the only followers of
the true Gospel. Then let them reply to the
Gospel. 'What I tell you in the darkness, utter
in the light, and what you hear whispered, pro-
claim from the housetops.'* You cannot re-   *Matt 10:27*
main silent any longer. How long will you keep
secret what God commands should be revealed?
How long is your gospel to remain hidden? It is
your gospel, I suspect, not St Paul's; he declares
that his is not hidden: 'If our gospel is a
mystery,' he says, 'it is only a mystery to
those on the way to perdition.'* Take care   *2 Cor 4:3*
that it is not you he speaks of, when it is
found that your gospel is hidden. Is it not
all too clear that you are on the way to perdition? Perhaps you do not even accept St Paul?
I have heard that that is true of some of you.
Yet you do not all agree about everything,
even if you all disagree with us.

4. Yet, if I am not mistaken, you all
accept without question the words, the writ-
ings, and the traditions of those who lived in
the bodily presence of the Saviour. Did these
men keep their gospel hidden? Were they
silent about the weakness of the flesh in God
Incarnate, the horror of his death, the degra-
dation of his cross? Indeed, their voice goes
out through all the world.* Where is the   *Ps 18:5*
apostolic pattern of life of which you boast?

They shout their teaching; you whisper; they
in public, you in corners; they fly like a
Is 60:8   cloud, you lurk in the darkness, in holes
under ground. What likeness do you bear to
them? Perhaps the fact that you take women
2 Tim 3:6   not as travelling companions but as mis-
tresses? Companionship does not lay itself
open to suspicion in the same was as living
together. Who would entertain dark suspicions
about those who raised the dead to life? Go
Lk 10:37   and do likewise, and I will suppose that a
man and a woman together are merely resting.
Otherwise, you are insolently abrogating to
yourself the privilege of those whose sanctity
you do not possess. To be always in a woman's
company without having carnal knowledge of
her—is this not a greater miracle than raising
the dead? You cannot perform the lesser feat;
do you expect me to believe that you can do
the greater? Every day your side touches the
girl's side at table, your bed touches hers in
your room, your eyes meet hers in conversation, your hands meet hers at work—do you
expect to be thought chaste? It may be that
you are, but I have my suspicions. To me
you are an object of scandal. Take away the
cause of scandal, and prove the truth of your
boast that you are a follower of the Gospel.
Does the Gospel not condemn the man who
Matt 18:6   offends someone within the Church? You
scandalize the Church; you are a fox who
spoils the vine. Help me, friends, to catch
him; better yet, holy angels, you catch him
for us. He is very cunning, he is covered with
Ps 72:6   unrighteousness and impiety; he is evidently
so small, so subtle, that he can easily deceive

the eyes of men. Is he to deceive yours too? It is to you, as companions of the Bridegroom, that these words are addressed. 'Catch us the little foxes.'* Do as you are bidden, then; catch this deceptive little fox for me, this little fox which we have long pursued in vain. Teach us, suggest to us how his trickery may be found out. Then the fox will be caught, for a dishonest Catholic does far more harm than an honest heretic. It is not for man to know what is in man,* unless he is enlightened for this very purpose by the Spirit of God or guided by angelic activity. What sign will you give us, that this vile heresy may be brought into the open, this heresy which knows so well how to dissemble not only with its tongue but in its life.

5. Indeed, when a vine has been spoilt this is a sign that a fox has been there. But the creature is very cunning and conceals his own footprints by some unknown artifice, so that no-one can easily discover how he goes in and out. Though his work is visible, its author is nowhere to be seen; he is completely hidden under the havoc he has caused. In fact, if you question him about his faith, nothing could be more orthodox; if [you question him] as to his way of life, nothing could be more irreproachable; and he proves his words by his deeds. What you see is a man frequenting the church, honoring the clergy, offering his gifts, making his confession, receiving the sacraments. What can be more orthodox. As far as his life and conduct are concerned he harms no-one, distresses no-one, does not set himself above anyone.* His face is pale from

*Sg 2:15

*Jn 2:25

*Lk 3:14

Prov 31:27

1 Thess 4:11

Matt 7:16

fasting, he does not eat the bread of idleness,* he supports himself with the labor of his hands.* Where is your fox now? We had him in our power a moment ago. How has he slipped from our hands? How did he disappear so suddenly? We must go after him, dig him out. By his fruits we shall know him;* and certainly spoilt vines point to a fox. Women have left their husbands, and husbands their wives, to join these people. Clerks and priests, young and old, have left their people and their churches, and are to be found there among weavers and their women. Is this not great havoc? Is this not the work of foxes?

6. But they do not all perform these overt actions, or if they do it cannot be proved. How then are we to catch them? Let us return to the question of associating and cohabiting with women, for all of them have some experience of this. 'Now, my good man, who is this woman, and where does she come from? Is she your wife?' 'No,' he says, 'that is forbidden by my vows.' 'Your daughter then?' 'No.' 'What then? Not a sister or niece, or at least related to you by birth or marriage?' 'No, not at all,' 'And how will you preserve your chastity with her here? You can't behave like this. Perhaps you don't know that the Church forbids cohabitation of men and women if they are vowed to celibacy. If you do not wish to cause scandal in the Church, send the woman away. Otherwise that one circumstance will give rise to other suspicions, which may not be proved but will no doubt be thought probable.'

7. 'But,' he says, 'can you show me any

passage in the Gospel forbidding this?' 'You have appealed to the Gospel; to the Gospel you shall go.* If you obey the Gospel, you will not cause scandal, for the Gospel clearly forbids you to do so.* But this is what you are doing, by disobeying the precept of the Church. You had been under suspicion, but now you will be openly censured as one who scorns the Gospel and as an enemy of the Church.'

What is your opinion, brothers? If he remains obdurate, and refuses to obey the Gospel* or to assent to the Church's teaching, how can you hesitate? Is it not obvious to you that the trickery is found out and the fox caught? If he does not remove the woman he does not remove the scandal; if he does not remove the scandal when he can remove it, he is clearly disobedient to the Gospel. What is the Church to do but remove the man who will not remove the scandal, unless, like him, she is to be disobedient?* For she has this command from the Gospel, not to spare her own eye if it gives offence, or her hand, or her foot, but to pluck it out or cut it off and cast it away from her.* 'If he will not listen to the Church,' it says, 'let him be to you as a stranger and a tax collector.'*

8. Have we accomplished anything? I think we have. We have caught the fox, we have unmasked his deception; those false Catholics who have lurked unseen have been disclosed in their true colors as plunderers of the Church. For while he was taking sweet food with me—I mean the Body and the Blood of Christ—while we walked in the house

Ac 25:12

Matt 18:6-7

Rom 10:16

Jn 8:55

Matt 5:29

Matt 18:17

of God as friends,* there occurred an opportunity for persuasion, or rather an occasion for perversion, in accordance with the saying of Wisdom: A hypocrite with his mouth destroys his neighbor;* but now, following Paul's wisdom, I shall without hesitation reject a heretic after a first and second admonition,* knowing that such a man is corrupt, and that I must take care he does not corrupt me also. It is therefore no mean achievement that, in the words of Wisdom, the treacherous shall be taken captive by their lust,* and especially those treacherous men who deliberately employ weapons of deception. For they avoid any open conflict and defence. They are indeed a base and uncouth race, unlettered and wholly lacking in courage. In short, they are foxes, and little ones. The points in which we allege they are mistaken are indefensible, and not so much subtle as plausible, and then only to peasant girls and imbeciles, such as are all I have met of this way of thinking. I do not recall having heard anything in all their many statements which made any contribution to knowledge, but only trite sayings well-aired by heretics of old, yet crushed and exploded by our theologians. It should be said, however—and I will say it— how absurd these statements are. Some of them they have formulated in the course of drawing ill-considered conclusions from discussions between Catholics; some they have produced in arguments with each other; some have been reported to us by a number of them who have returned to the Church. I say this not because I intend to reply to them

Prov 11:9

Tit 3:10

Prov 11:6

all—that would be unnecessary—but just so
that they may be noticed. But this will be the
subject of another sermon, to the praise and
glory of the name of the Bridegroom of the
Church,* Jesus Christ our Lord, who is above   *Ps 78:9
all, God blessed for ever.* Amen.   *Rom 9:5

One of Bernard's sources of information about the Cathari was Eberwin
of Steinfeld, prior of a praemonstratensian community near Cologne.
Between 1140 and 1143, Eberwin wrote to the abbot, hoping apparently to induce Bernard to speak out again heretical groups of
laymen in and around Cologne. The text of his letter is found in
PL 182:676-80. An English translation appears in Peter Allix and
Samuel Roffrey Maitland, *Facts and Documents Illustrative of the
History, Doctrine, and Rites, of the Ancient Albigenses and Waldenses*
(London:Rivington, 1832) 344-350; reprinted in Jeffrey Burton Rus-
sell, *Religious Dissent in the Middle Ages* (New York: Wiley, 1971)
60–63.

SERMON SIXTY-SIX

I. MORE ABOUT THESE NEW HERETICS,
THAT THEY ARE THE ONES OF WHOM
THE APOSTLE SAID ESPECIALLY THAT
THEY SPEAK LIES IN HYPOCRISY.
II. HOW THEY SCORN MARRIAGE AND
MANY OF THEM RETIRE WITH VIRGINS
ALONE. III. THE FOODS THEY CON-
SIDER UNCLEAN AND HOW THEY SAY
THEY MAKE UP THE BODY OF CHRIST
AND CALL THEMSELVES APOSTLES.
IV. ARGUMENTS AGAINST THE STATE-
MENT THAT INFANTS SHOULD NOT BE
BAPTISED, THE DEAD NOT PRAYED FOR,
THE INTERCESSION OF THE SAINTS NOT
SOUGHT. V. ARGUMENTS AGAINST
THEIR SCORN FOR THE ORDERS AND
STATUTES OF THE CHURCH AND THEIR
OBSTINENT CONVICTION OF BEING
MURDERED FOR THEIR SECT.

*Sg 2:15

*Ps 79:13

I. 1. 'CATCH US THE LITTLE FOXES that spoil the vines.'* I am still on the foxes. They are those who strip the vines as they go along the path.* Not content with turning aside from the way, they must also make a desert of the vineyard by indulging in falsehoods. It is not enough to be heretics, they must also be

190

hypocrites, adding sin to sin beyond measure?* They are those who come in sheep's clothing, to strip the sheep and despoil the rams.* Do you not see how these purposes are fulfilled, when we find the people robbed of their faith and the priests of their people? Who are these robbers? In appearance they are sheep, in cunning they are foxes, but in their cruel deeds they are wolves. They wish to appear good without being so, and to be evil without appearing so. But they are evil, and only desire to appear good that they may not be alone in their evil. They are afraid to appear evil, lest they prove less than evil. For malice has always less power to harm when it is obvious; no good man is ever deceived except by a pretence of goodness. It is to cause the downfall of the good that they strive to appear good; they avoid the appearance of evil so that their malice may have full play. It is not their nature to foster virtues, but to gloss over their vices with a veneer of virtue. Then they honor their blasphemy with the name of religion. Innocence they define as doing no open harm, so that it is only the appearance of innocence that they make their own. To hide their immorality they take a vow of chastity. Moreover, they suppose immorality consists only in taking a wife, whereas marriage is the only condition which justifies sexual intercourse.* They are coarse and ignorant, and altogether contemptible. But they must not be dismissed lightly, I assure you, for they will become more and more ungodly, and their talk will slither along like cancer.*

*Deut 9:12, 16

*Rom 7:13

*Matt 19:10

*2 Tim 2:16

2. Indeed they have not been overlooked by the Holy Spirit, since he has plainly prophesied about them, saying by the Apostle: 'Now the Spirit says openly that in later times some will depart from the faith, heeding deceitful spirits and the doctrines of demons, through the pretension of liars whose consciences are seared, who forbid marriage and enjoin abstinence from foods which God created to be received with thanksgiving.'* These are clearly the people to whom he refers. They forbid marriage, they abstain from foods which God has created—this matter I will examine later. But now consider whether this is not a machination of demons rather than a human error, as the Spirit foretold. Inquire of them who the founder of their sect is; they will not give a name. When has there been a heresy of human origin without its own leader? The Manichees had Manes for their leader and teacher, the Sabellians had Sabellius, the Arians Arius, the Eunomians Eunomius, and the Nestorians Nestorius. So also with other such scourges, each has its own acknowledged leader from whom it takes its origin and name. What name or title will you ascribe to these men? Surely their heresy is not of human origin, nor did they receive it from a human being.* God forbid that we should regard it as a revelation of Jesus Christ—let us rather see it, without any question, as the Holy Spirit foretold, as a deceitful suggestion of demons, a deceitful hypocrisy of lying hypocrites who forbid marriage.* They say this as hypocrites, with the cunning of foxes, pretending that their

1 Tim 4:1-3

Gal 1:12

1 Tim 4:1-3

words are inspired by a love of chastity, whereas their motive is rather to foment and increase immorality. This is so obvious that I wonder how any Christian could be taken in by it, unless there are people so stupid that they do not perceive how a man who condemns marriage opens the door to every kind of impurity, or so full of wickedness and soaked in devilish malice that they deny the evidence of their eyes and rejoice in men's ruin.*

Wis 1:13

II. Take from the Church the honourable estate of marriage and the purity of the marriage-bed,* and you will surely fill it with concubinage, incest, masturbation, effeminacy, homosexuality—in short, with every kind of filthiness.* Choose then which you prefer: that all who practise these enormities should be saved, or only the few who are chaste. How few are to be classed with the latter, how many with the former! Our Lord and Saviour does not desire either of these ends. Shall immorality receive a crown? There is nothing more difficult to reconcile with the purity of God. Is the whole world to be condemned apart from a few who are chaste? It is not the nature of our Saviour to act like this. On earth, chastity is rare; but the fulness of grace has not wasted away because the harvest is so small.* How indeed could we all have received of that fulness* if it were only the chaste who were allowed to share it? This reasoning cannot be disproved, there can be no reply to this. Nor, I think, to the other. If there is a place in heaven for righteousness,

Heb 13:14

1 Cor 6:10

Phil 2:7
Jn 1:11

yet there is no fellowship between the righteous and the base, just as there is no frater-
nization between light and darkness* then
certainly there is no place in the scheme of
salvation for any who are unclean.* If anyone
should think otherwise, let him be persuaded
by the voice of the Apostle, who declares
without any ambiguity: 'Those who do such
things shall not inherit the Kingdom of
God.'* How shall this cunning little fox now
creep out of his hole? I think he is caught in
his own lair; in it he has made, so to speak,
two funnels for himself, one to go in by, and
one to go out of. This is his habit. Now see
how both ways of escape are closed to him;
for if he puts only the chaste in heaven, salvation ceases to exist for most people; if however he puts every kind of filthiness on a par
with chastity, then righteousness ceases to
exist. But it would be more accurate to say
that he himself ceases to exist, for he cannot
escape by either way, but is shut up for ever,
caught in the pit he dug himself.*

4. But there are some, differing from the
rest, who maintain that marriages may take
place, but only between virgins. I cannot see
on what reasonable grounds they make this
distinction, unless it be that they all at their
pleasure jostle each other in their struggle to
tear apart the sacraments of the Church with
their poisoned fangs, those sacraments which
are, as it were, their mother's womb. For
when they allege, as they apparently do, that
our first parents were virgins, how can this
possibly affect the freedom of marriage in
such a way that it cannot be contracted

*2 Cor 6:14

*Phil 3:15

*Gal 5:21

*Ps 7:16

between those who are not virgins? But they mumble that they have found something or other in the Gospel which they mistakenly suppose gives credence to their absurdities. I suppose that they mean the statement in Genesis that 'God created man in his own image and likeness, male and female created he them'* was followed by Our Lord's saying 'Therefore what God has joined together let no man put asunder'.* 'God joined them together,' they say, 'because they were both virgins, and they could not subsequently be lawfully separated; but the union of those who are not virgins shall not be presumed to be of God.' 'But who has told you that their virginity was the reason for their marriage? This is not what the Scriptures say.' 'But were they not virgins?' you say. Indeed they were; but the marriage of people who are virgins is not the same thing as the marriage of people because they are virgins. Even so, you will not find it expressly stated that they were virgins, although they were. It is the difference in sex which is meant by the saying 'Male and female created he them,'* not virginity; and rightly so, for it is the difference in sex which is the essential element in marriage, not physical virginity! Rightly then, when marriage was instituted, the Holy Spirit spoke of the distinction of sex, but made no mention of virginity. He left no trail for cunning little foxes to follow. They would readily have done so, though without result. But if he had said 'He created them virgins' would you then have immediately inferred that only virgins marry? What capital you would have made

*Gen 1:27

*Mk 10:10

*Gen 1:27

out of that one statement! What denunciations you would have uttered about second and third marriages! How you would have reviled the Catholic Church for being prepared to marry prostitutes and panderers, inasmuch as she is ready to believe that they are abandoning an immoral way of life for an honorable one! Perhaps you· would also find fault with God for commanding the Prophet [Hosea] to marry a whore? But as it is you have no pretext, and elect to be a heretic for no apparent reason. And the argument you use to fabricate* your error appears more likely to destroy it. It does not strengthen your case but greatly weakens it.

5. Now hear a text which will either confound you utterly or correct you, and which completely crushes and destroys your heresy. 'A wife is bound to her husband as long as he lives; but if the husband die, she is free to marry whoever she chooses, in the Lord.'* It is Paul who permits a widow to marry whomever she chooses and you contradict this and say that no woman except a virgin may marry, and then only to a virgin and not to whomever she chooses. Why do you shorten God's arm?* Why do you limit the abundant blessings of marriage? Why do you restrict to a virgin the right which is granted to all her sex? Paul would not permit it unless it were lawful. But 'permit' is an understatement; he also commends it. 'I wish,' he says, 'the younger women to marry,'* and there is no doubt that he includes widows. What could be clearer? What he permits, then, because it is lawful, he also commends because it is expedient.* Is a here-

*SBOp has
destruendum
*but the sense
demands*
struendum
—trans.

*Dan 2:40,
1 Cor 7:39

*Is 59:1

*1 Tim 5:14

*1 Cor 6:12

tic to forbid what is both lawful and expedient? He will persuade no one of anything by
his prohibition, except that he is a heretic.

III. 6. There remains some criticism to be
made about these men because of the rest of
the Apostle's words, for, as he predicted, they
abstain from foods which God ordained to be
received with thanksgiving,* thus proving them- *1 Tim 4:3*
selves to be heretics, not for their abstinence
in itself but for the heretical spirit in which
they undertake it. I myself practise abstinence
from time to time, but my abstinence is a re-
paration for sin, not a scrupulous observance
devoid of reverence. Are we to censure Paul for
disciplining his body and bringing it into subjection?* I will abstain from wine because in *1 Cor 9:27*
drinking wine there is the possibility of excess;* *Eph 5:18*
but if I am weak I will use it sparingly, following the apostle's counsel.* I will abstain from *1 Tim 5:23*
flesh meats, lest they over-stimulate the flesh
and with it the lusts of the flesh. I will be at
pains to take even bread in moderation, lest
because of a loaded stomach I get tired of standing to pray, and lest the prophet [Ezekiel]
bring this reproach upon me also, that I gorge
myself with bread.* I will not even get into *Ezek 16:49*
the habit of gulping down pure water, lest
fulness of the stomach lead to the stimulation
of desire. It is not so with the heretic. He
avoids milk, and everything made from it, and
even goes so far as to refuse any food which is
produced by copulation. This would be a
right and christian course of action if it were
taken not because such things were the result
of copulation but so that they might not
become its cause.

7. But what is the reason for this whole-sale avoidance of everything produced by copulation? This close scrutiny of food, these detailed instructions, arouse my suspicions. If you commend it to us on medical grounds, we will not censure you for taking care of your body—for no one ever hates his body*—provided it is done in moderation. If you give as your reason the disciplinary value of abstinence, that is the routine of spiritual therapy, we will even approve it as laudable, so long as by bringing the flesh into subjection you curb its lusts. But if you limit the goodness of God after the insane manner of the Manichaean, so that what he has created and given to be received with thankfulness,* you, ungrateful, thoughtless and censorious, judge to be unclean and shun like the plague, then I certainly do not commend your abstinence. On the contrary, I condemn your blasphemy. I am inclined to say that it is you who are unclean, when you brand anything as unclean in itself. 'To the pure all things are pure,'* says one who is a clear thinker. Nothing is unclean except to one who thinks it unclean. 'But to the corrupt and the unbeliever nothing is pure; their very minds and consciences are corrupted.' Woe to you who spew out of your mouth the very food which God has created, considering it too unclean and unworthy for you to absorb into your own body. But it is you, polluted and unclean, who are spewed out by the Body of Christ, which is the Church.*

8. I am not unaware of their boast that they, and they alone, are the Body of Christ.

*Eph 5:29

*1 Tim 4:3-4

*Tit 1:15

*Col 1:24

But since they believe this, they must also believe that they have the power of consecrating the Body and Blood of Christ on their altars every day, to nourish them to become members of the Body of Christ. To be sure, they confidently claim to be the successors of the Apostles, and call themselves apostolic, although they are unable to show any sign of their apostolate. How long is their light to remain under a bushel? 'You are the light of the world'*—this was said to the Apostles, therefore the Apostles are set on a candlestick, to give light to the whole world. The successors of the Apostles should be ashamed to be the light, not of the world, but only of a bushel,* so that they are the darkness of the world. Let us say to them: 'You are the darkness of the world,' and pass on to other matters. They claim to be the Church, but they contradict the saying of Our Lord, 'A city set on a hill cannot be hid'.* Do you believe that the stone which, being cut from the mountain by no human hand, itself became the mountain and filled the world* is shut up in your caverns? They do not seek to make known their opinions; it is enough to mutter in private. Christ holds his heritage undiminished, and will always do so, and the ends of the earth are his possession.* They take themselves out of this mighty heritage when they try to take it from Christ.*
9. Look at those detractors. Look at those dogs.

IV. They ridicule us for baptising infants, praying for the dead, and asking the prayers

*Matt 5:15

*Matt 5:14

*Ibid.

*Dan 2:34

*Ps 2:8

*Phil 3:2

of the saints. They lose no time in cutting Christ off from all kinds of people to both sexes, young and old, living and dead. They put infants outside the sphere of grace because they are too young to receive it, and those who are full grown because they find difficulty in preserving chastity. They deprive the dead of the help of the living, and rob the living of the prayers of the saints because they have died. God forbid! The Lord will not forsake his people* who are as the sands of the sea,† nor will he who redeemed all be content with a few, and those heretics. For his redemptive grace is not a trifling thing; it is very plenteous.* How can the small number of these men be matched with the greatness of the prize? They cheat themselves of the prize when they empty it of its meaning. What does it matter if a child cannot speak for himself? The voice of the blood of his brother—and of such a brother—cries out to God from the ground.* His mother the Church also stands by his side and cries out. And what of the child himself? Does he not seem to you somehow to be looking with longing for the wells of salvation?* Do you not think you hear him crying out to God and calling out in his whimperings, 'Lord, I suffer violence; answer for me'*? He demands the help of grace because he suffers violence from nature. It is the innocence of the poor child which cries out; it is his ignorance; it is the weakness of one doomed to die. All these cry out— his brother's blood, the devotion of his mother, the helplessness of an unhappy child, and the unhappiness of a helpless one. Their

*Kgs 12:22
†Gen 32:12

*Ps 129:7

*Gen 4:10

*Is 12:3

*Is 38:14

crying rises to the Father. Now the Father
cannot act unlike himself; he is a father.

10.   Let no one tell me that a child has no
faith, for his mother imparts her own to him,
wrapping him in the sacrament of baptism as
in a cloak, until he is ready to embrace it in its
purity and fulness,* if not by his own   *Is 28:20*
experience, yet by conscious assent. It would
be a narrow garment which could not cover
both of them. But the faith of the Church is
wide. Is it less than that of the Canaanite
woman, which was certainly wide enough to
cover herself and her child? Consequently the
answer she heard was: 'Woman, great is your
faith. Be it done for you as you desire.'* Is it   *Matt 15:28*
less than the faith of those who let the
paralytic down through the roof, gaining for
him health of mind and body? When he saw
their faith, he said to the paralytic: 'Have
faith; your sins are forgiven',* and a little   *Mk 2:5*
later 'Take up your bed and walk'.* He who   *Ibid.*
believes these things will easily be persuaded
that the Church is right to claim salvation for
children baptized in her faith, and the crown
of martyrdom for the infants who were
killed for Christ. This being so, those who
are re-born in baptism will take no harm from
the saying: 'Without faith it is impossible to
please God',* since those who have received   *Heb 11:6*
the grace of baptism to witness to their
faith* are not without faith, nor will they   *Heb 11:39*
suffer ill from that other text: 'He who does
not believe shall be lost',* for what is believ-   *Mk 16:16*
ing but having faith? So a woman shall be
saved by child-bearing if she continues in
faith;* children shall be strengthened by the   *1 Tim 2:15*

new birth of baptism; grown men who cannot preserve their continence* shall redeem themselves by the thirtyfold fruit of marriage.* Through the mediation of angels, the dead shall profit by the prayers and sacrifices of the living, of which they have needed and to which they have a right. Those who are still on the way shall lack no manner of consolation from those whose course here is done. Through God, who is everywhere, and in God, they shall lack no kind of love and compassion from those who are not physically present with them. For this is why Christ died and rose again, that he might be Lord of the living and the dead.* This is why he was born as an infant and advanced to manhood through all the stages of life, so that he might not be lacking to any stage.

11. They do not believe that there remains after death the fire of purgatory, but allege that when the soul is released from the body it passes straight to rest or to damnation. Let them ask of him who said that there was a sin which should not be forgiven in this world nor in the world to come.*

V. Now it is not to be wondered at if those who do not acknowledge the Church decry her statutes, reject her ordinances, regard the sacraments with contempt and refuse to obey her precepts. The successors of the Apostles, they say, are sinners, whether they are archbishops, bishops, or priests, and are fit therefore neither to administer nor to receive the Sacraments; for to be a bishop is incompatible with being a sinner. This is untrue. Caiaphas

was a bishop,* and what a great sinner he was, ***Jn 11:50**
pronouncing the sentence of death on Our
Lord. If you say he was not a bishop, the witness of John will confound you, for he records
that he prophesied in the year that he was
High Priest.* Judas was an apostle, and chosen ***Jn 11:51**
by the Lord, even if he was covetous and
wicked. Or have you doubts about the apostolate of someone the Lord chose? 'Have I not
chosen you twelve,' he said, 'and one of you
is a devil?'* You hear that he was chosen as ***Jn 6:71**
an apostle and proved himself a devil, and yet
you deny that a man who is a sinner can be a
bishop? The Scribes and Pharisees sat in
Moses' seat,* and those who did not give them ***Matt 23:3**
the obedience due to bishops were guilty of
disobedience, for the Lord himself gave this
command when he said: 'Whatever they say,
do it.'* It is clear then that although they ***Ibid.**
were Scribes and Pharisees, although they were
great sinners, yet because of the seat of Moses,
the saying which he uttered applies to them:
'He that hears you hears me; he that despises
you despises me.'* ***Lk 10:16**

12. Many other persuasive arguments are
adduced by lying and hypocritical spirits to de-
ceive these dull-witted and foolish people,* but ***Jn 20:30, Deut**
it is not necessary to answer all of them. For **32:6, 1 Tim 4:11,**
who can perceive all of them? Besides, it would **Ps 5:7**
be an endless task and quite unnecessary. For
these men are not to be convinced by logical
reasoning, which they do not understand, nor
prevailed upon by references to authority,
which they do not accept, nor can they be won
over by persuasive arguments, for they are
utterly perverted. This is indisputable, for they

*Phil 3:19

*Judg 15:4

*The accused
would be thrown
into a body of
water. If he sank,
his innocence
was proclaimed;
if he floated, his
guilt was
assumed.
IV Lateran
(1215) forbade
priests to take
part in such
trials by ordeal,
preferring the
less spectacular
system of trial
by law.

*Rom 13:4

prefer death to conversion.* The end of these men is destruction, fire awaits them at the last. They are prefigured in Samson's exploit of setting fire to the tails of foxes.* Often the faithful have seized some of them and brought them before a tribunal. When questioned on the points of their belief which are suspect, they have denied everything completely, as they always do, and when examined by the ordeal of water† they have been found to be lying. But when detected and unable to make any further denial because the water would not receive them, they have taken the bit between their teeth, as the saying is, and instead of confessing their blasphemy freely and with penitence, they have declared it openly, alleging that it was true piety, and for it they have been ready to suffer death, which those standing by have been equally ready to inflict. So people have attacked them, making new martyrs for the cause of godless heresy. We applaud their zeal, but do not recommend their action, because faith should be a matter of persuasion, not of force, though no doubt it is better for them to be restrained by the sword of someone who bears not the sword in vain* than to be allowed to lead others into heresy. Anyone who punishes a wrong-doer in righteous wrath is a servant of God.

13. It is surprising to some people that they meet their death not only with patience, but also, apparently, joyfully. But they do not take into consideration the mighty power of the devil not only over men's bodies, but also over their hearts. Once he is admitted, he will take possession. Is it not more surprising

that a man should lay violent hands on himself than that he should suffer violence willingly at the hands of another? Yet we have frequently seen the devil exercising this power over many who have drowned themselves or hanged themselves. Indeed, there is no doubt that it was at the devil's suggestion that Judas hanged himself.* But I find it much more surprising that he could put it into the heart of Judas to betray the Lord* than suggest to him that he hang himself. The obstinacy of these men has nothing in common with the constancy of the martyrs; for they were endowed by their piety with a contempt for death, whereas these others are prompted by their hardness of heart. Thus the Prophet, speaking perhaps with the voice of a martyr, says 'Their heart is as fat as butter, but I have meditated on the law',* meaning that, although the suffering looks the same, the intention is very different, for the one hardened his heart against God,* whereas the other meditated on the law of the Lord.*

*Matt 27:5

*Jn 13:2

*Ps 118:70

*2 Chron 36:13
*Ps 1:2

14. It is unnecessary and useless, therefore, to utter long tirades against these foolish and obstinate men. It is enough that they should be known for what they are, so that you may be on your guard against them. They should be dealt with, then, either by being forced to send away their women or to leave the Church, as they cause scandal in the Church by their way of life and their consorting with women. It is regretable that not only distinguished laymen but also some of the clergy—even some of episcopal rank—who should rather have been seeking them

out, give them support for payment, and
accept presents from them. 'But,' they say,
'how are we to condemn men who have
neither been convicted of error nor admit
it?' This is nonsense, not so much a reason as
an excuse. They can easily be dealt with by
this means, if by no other. As I have said, you
must separate the men from the women,
although they claim they are living chaste
lives, and require the women to live with
others of their sex who are under similar
vows, and similarly men with men of the same
way of life. In this way you will protect the
vows and reputations of both, and they will
have you as witnesses and guardians of their
chastity. If they do not accept this, you will
be completely justified in expelling them from
the Church to which they have caused scandal
by their blatant and illicit cohabitation. Let
Lk 1:77   these measures suffice to trap the little foxes*
in their cunning, and to edify and protect
the beloved and glorious Bride of Our Lord
Rom 9:5   Jesus Christ,* who is God above all,
blessed for ever.
Amen.

ABBREVIATIONS

CCSL	*Corpus Christianorum Series Latina.* Turnhout, Belgium. 1953–
CF	Cistercian Fathers Series
Dil	Bernard of Clairvaux, *De diligendo Deo (On Loving God)*
D Sp	Dictionnaire de Spiritualité. Paris. 1953–
PL	J. P. Migne, Patrologiae cursus completus, series latina. Rpt. Paris, 1957–64.
RB	*Regula monachorum sancti Benedicti (Rule of St Benedict)*
SBOp	*Sancti Bernardi Opera,* edd. J. Leclercq, H. M. Rochais, C. H. Talbot. Rome, 1957–
SC	Bernard of Clairvaux, *Sermones super Cantica Canticorum (Sermons on the Song of Songs)*
Spec fid	William of St Thierry, *Speculum fidei (The Mirror of Faith)*

Psalms have been cited according to the Vulgate enumeration.